IN MEDIAS RES

IN MEDIAS RES

Liturgy for the Estranged

Catherine Madsen

The Davies Group, Publishers
Aurora, Colorado

Library of Congress Cataloging-in-Publication Data

Madsen, Catherine, 1952-
  In medias res : liturgy for the estranged / Catherine Madsen.
    p. cm.
  Includes bibliographical references.
  ISBN 978-1-934542-01-9 (alk. paper)
  1. Ritual. 2. Rites and ceremonies. I. Title.
  BL600.M25 2008
  203'.8--dc22
                                              2007050687

Cover and author photos by J. M. Boucher

Printed in the United States of America

0987654321

for Judith Anderson
1934 – 2008

Contents

Author's Note, 2007

Anyone who writes a deliberately controversial book about the failures of modern liturgy should be expected to follow it with a book that shows how the job should be done. This is not that book. *In Medias Res* was written some fifteen years before *The Bones Reassemble*, when I had only begun to feel my way toward the premises for liturgical writing that I set out there. I was in the fairly common position of being unable to accept any of the revelations on offer, but not wanting to live without shared ritual; I drew from the only scriptures I had, the poetry and prose I trusted, to imagine what that ritual might be. There are certainly things here that I would no longer write—and I could prove by my own methods how much of it is not worth repeating—but the approach may still be useful to other liturgists.

At the risk of redundancy I have retained the original preface, which discusses my use of quotation. I have also added introductory comments to each ritual. A few general remarks may help to place the whole enterprise on the religious spectrum. The rituals are "secular" in the sense that they assume no necessary connection between ritual and theism, and "pagan" in the sense that they take the seasons for their calendar. In some underlying sense they are Jewish, or proto-Jewish, in their reaching for what Emmanuel Levinas called a religion for adults. They assume the inadequacy of faith—both ethically and practically—to sustain itself after the various moral and humanitarian disasters committed in its name, and also the inadequacy of reason—both ethically and aesthetically—to provide a new liturgical center. It may be unfair to call the ideological massacres of the twentieth century *worse* than the Inquisition or the upheavals of the Reformation, as if secularity had finally stripped the gloves off human barbarism; every age does its best with the technology it has. But reason has not supplied a reliably humane alternative to faith, or even managed to show a clear link between belief and behavior. My own sense is that the point of ritual is not to set forth a coherent theology or ideology at all, but to create a state of mind. The aphorisms in the section "Prometheus Stealing Torah for the People" are my initial attempts to understand how this state of mind might work.

Aidan Kavanagh, in *On Liturgical Theology,* suggests that theology derives from worship, not the other way round: that the liturgical *practice* of the "human assembly," for whom worship is "vertiginous, on the edge of chaos," changes their lives subtly and gradually, and that subsequent repetitions of the liturgy absorb these changes in experiential rather than analytical form. This process, with its natural fluctuations of eagerness and reluctance, trust and mistrust, Kavanagh calls "primary theology." Academic or secondary theology, however absorbing a discipline in its own right, is ancillary; if it is systematically imposed on liturgy, it prematurely stabilizes the vertigo and stands between the assembly and its experience. A liturgical cycle that springs full-blown from one writer's mind cannot hope to duplicate a group process that evolves over hundreds of years, but the use of quotation makes it in a sense collaborative; the presence of voices from several centuries suggests historical continuity, while at the same time disrupting any philosophical coherence that might try to form.

My own desire for shared ritual began during three childhood years in a harsh northern climate, where nothing that offered itself as religion was adequate to the experience—personal or social—of the climate itself. I eventually found common ground with other people not so much in the details of the experience as in its intensity: the heightened perception of common objects and occasions that accompanies disruption, responsibility and risk. People have told me of having had that experience after the death of a lover, after an episode of madness, after being violently attacked; Rilke speaks of something like it in the Ninth Duino Elegy when he commands us to *sprich und bekenn*, "speak and bear witness":

> Perhaps we are *here* in order to say: house,
> bridge, fountain, gate, pitcher, fruit-tree, window—
> at most: column, tower.... But to *say* them, you must under-
> stand,
> oh to say them *more* intensely than the Things themselves
> ever dreamed of existing.

This is Stephen Mitchell's translation, a little breathless like Rilke's original, but nonetheless an accurate enough record of the experience. When language reaches us at a vertiginous time it comes, as it were, in italics. This kind of heightened perception is prior to ritual, and is profoundly private; it is not concerned with Kavanagh's human assembly, and is even in flight from it. But ritual echoes what happens when two or three people acquainted with vertigo are gathered together; it brings our human obligations into contact with our inmost passivities in a paradox of participation and privacy.

The great liturgies of the West evolved from a crisis of loss, and from the need to establish a collective form of endurance in the face of the loss. They consolidated a shared experience into a body of ritual, part of whose purpose was to regenerate heightened perception. The Christian liturgy enacts the appearance, the disappearance through death, the miraculous reappearance through resurrection, and the second disappearance through ascension, of God in human flesh. The communion aims to make him present to believers in his prolonged absence as plain physical and spiritual sustenance, food and drink. The liturgy of rabbinic Judaism aims to replace the sacrifices of the destroyed Temple with a sacrifice of the heart so thoroughgoing, so rooted in home and body, that

the Jewish people's conviction of election and liberation will persist, and the people cohere and proliferate, even in prolonged exile.
From the outside—even from the inside, in times of spiritual tor-
por—worship can look tedious; Elias Canetti called religion a "slow
crowd" for its prolongation of the normally more vibrant or violent
experience of forming an assembly. But liturgy worth repeating
always has in it the seeds, the triggers, of the vertigo. Embedded
in a mass of words and acts that are more or less unchanging is a
profound sense of contingency, more or less shared by all the participants. The details of our vulnerability differ by century and ge-
ography, but we are all breakable and all under sentence of death.
The slowness of liturgy may not be tedium but a sort of tantric
intimacy, in which God (an invisible and imperceptible God) and
the assembly hold each other in the vertigo for solace.

In the West in the last few centuries, those who are estranged from religion have found one possible alternative in
the direct experience of nature. This is often, as in my own
case, a kind of pantheism without the theism, having a scientific, emotional, or mythological inflection depending on the
individual temperament. The Enlightenment idea of "natural
religion" saw common objects as intensely ordered by internal
law, by chemistry and physics unconditioned by scripture. The
Romantics' and the Transcendentalists' religion of nature allowed some role to disorder. As natural history and Darwinian
theory developed, they had cultural and spiritual repercussions
undreamt-of by either religion or scientific method. It was not
simply that the Enlightenment had let the air out of the balloon
of faith, but that we became conscious of our surroundings in
ways that religion had no means of coping with. (It still has
none; "ecotheology" struggles, but does not rise to the occasion.)
The sense of loss was present fairly early: English writers like
Blake, Wordsworth, Ruskin, George Eliot and Hardy saw the
threat posed by industrialization to a limited island landscape.

In North America, because the continent is so vast and was for a long time so sparsely populated, the pattern was different, but the discovery of a mighty landscape and the discovery of its fragility often went hand in hand. Loss now plays a rapidly accelerating part in our sense of the natural world. Pantheism in a time when great Pan is dead, or may be dying, is a different thing than a pantheism that happily throws off the religious burden of "guilt" in a return to the rural and bucolic. *Et in Arcadia ego*: the religion of nature rocks on its foundations with the irrecoverable shock of knowing that what one has taken innocently for granted—winter, the health of forests, the salinity of the oceans, polar ice—can no longer be counted upon.

There are still opinion columnists who write gleefully of climate change as a left-wing academic conspiracy or a liberal neurosis, and "environmentalism" as an upstart religion concocted by ignorant urbanites. Scientific models are never based on perfect knowledge, and scientists are as prone as any other theorists to errors of omission and commission; environmentalism, like any ism, has its share of callow fools and opportunists. Nonetheless, the permafrost is melting. Religions have always (so far) been wrong about their apocalypses, but the perennial human dread of apocalypse may have no bearing on the present case; science has often been right about its hypotheses. We must wait and see. But passive waiting is a horror to us; we want not only to refine our hypotheses but to influence events, to put back on course deliberately what we have derailed unintentionally. When in doubt, we would rather overestimate our influence than concede our helplessness. What puts my rituals very much in the mainstream of Western religion is their sense that our own natural actions can be a horror to us. If the Hebrew Bible makes a horror of our homely inclination toward animism, if Catholic teaching makes a horror of our sexual stirrings and our profane sense of humor, the religion of nature finds itself transfixed in dismay by our very metabolism: fire, the conversion of oxygen into carbon dioxide by our fuel, by our breath. Alas, Prometheus.

Jack Miles called a few years ago for a global requiem; I think we must imagine instead a global kaddish. The difference between the two is the difference between finality and recovery: a requiem mourns (once) and looks ahead to the end of the world, whereas a kaddish renegotiates (for months) our place in the world, accustoms us to the look of a world absent of our beloved. We are charged by our very habit of persistence with surviving the end of the world. Survival is not only a practical problem but an imaginative one; if our constitution compels us to survive, our consciousness has to discover what for.

Several readers have told me that the rituals are too "dark" and "heavy." No doubt they make difficult reading for those who think the purpose of ritual is to tell us we are OK. If liturgy cannot help us to face darkness, I wonder what it is for; surely part of its purpose has always been to precipitate and then to sustain us through lost innocence. The rituals of atonement and grief that are so tiresome to untroubled young people reveal themselves in their full necessity to the guilty and the bereft, to those who have a hard duty and those who are waiting for a diagnosis. Joy in ritual is greatly desirable, but it comes on the far side of fear and loss, not as a diversionary tactic; it is the return from exile, not the dance around the golden calf. If in any sense a return from exile awaits us, I stand ready to rejoice.

Catherine Madsen
September 2007

Preface, 1990

As a college student in the early seventies, I once attended a Lutheran service in the modern idiom, of which the only words I remember are "Lord of atom, earth and space." I remembered them because they seemed to be so modern as to be almost insincere—with the smiling, openhearted insincerity of a television host: an attempt to update the church's image with a casual assortment of items (small, medium and large) that sounded newsy and scientific. A writer who had sufficient awe of atoms or earth or space—or sufficient Lutheran fear of the Lord—would never have invoked all four of them in terms that sounded so much like dismissal. That leaden echo of biblical language has stood as a warning to me ever since of what the modern liturgist is up against.

I am not a Christian—not, of course, because of the hapless liturgist, but for more essential reasons—and the problem I am approaching is a somewhat different one. I am not attempting to make an old system palatable but to make certain thoughts sayable. I have written a liturgical cycle not of revelation but of experience and uncertainty. It is not intended to support the belief of a community of believers, but to offer an outline of public ritual to scattered and various people disaffected from belief. I began it in frustration at homemade weddings full of jargon and clichés, funerals that might have raised the dead through sheer embarrassment, and Christian and neopagan attempts to devise new rituals that left me wishing for the old ones. It was a rather practical matter at first (if any attempt to capture holiness can be said to be practical): certain public occasions did not seem to be effectual. I was not sure whether these occasions failed to be convincing because the participants were inarticulate and embarrassed, or whether their inarticulacy itself proceeded from a failure of conviction. I did sense that if care is not given to the purely theatrical aspects of ritual—timing, congruity, a choice of words as intense and concise as possible—those present will feel less like participants and more like an audience, and an audience that has been let down. So I did not begin with a spiritual motion like "Let everything that has breath praise the Lord," but with an exasperated "Good God, child, stand up straight and stick your stomach in!" Praise, like any other kind of potency, is impossible to the self-conscious; but once learn the habit of mind that makes it possible, and it will appear.

What many of these rituals wanted to praise—and this was half the reason for my impatience when they fell short—was the relations between people, and between people and the world. They did not look to an ineffable "beyond," and try to make its nature and its will explicable to the faithful; they looked at the imperfect and malleable "between," and tried to shape it. They looked for life to supply its own meaning. Though I disliked their means, I worked toward the same end. Everything comes out of the "between": ethics, stories, responsibility, paradox. It is almost as if, in the hurried and fragmented patterns of contemporary life, ordinary relations are the divine things that have been eclipsed, and that must be reiterated, recovered, insisted upon, prior to any theology. As if God must emerge from the spaces between us in order to be credible at all.

There is a slowing process, a withdrawal from casual talk, that helps this emergence. This is why the cadence and content of liturgical language matter: they help to establish trust, to loosen the hold of small-talk over people in groups. I have used a great deal of quotation in these rituals because it was language I trusted—a little of it biblical (which we are used to in liturgy) and much of it from secular poetry (which, for the most part, we are not). I have a particular object in mind with this combination. Poetry already functions as a kind of liturgy for those who take it seriously: as much as any psalm or commandment, it charges the reader to be faithful to some essential knowledge. Hopkins' "My own heart let me more have pity on," Rilke's "You must change your life," are more than observations of the human scene: they are morally binding. No one claims that poetry is revelation in the religious sense, or that its sources are anything but human and fallible. But poetry reminds us of what the stakes are, and sometimes it reminds us more effectively than religion. Religion has a system; one of its main cares is to safeguard its metaphors, to make sure its vocabulary is pure. It is not free to choose the language by which it reminds us. By mingling religious and secular quotations, without giving one precedence over the other, I hope to widen the range of what it is possible to think in each other's presence. This mingling may also give both forms a new kind of authority: not the authority of exhortation or of aesthetic judgment, but the authority of a continuing conversation whose motives we trust—a conditional but quite genuine authority.

I've wondered since childhood why people place religious authority in titles and offices rather than in the behavior of people they trust; surely it's these people who make authority credible at all. In the end all authority is conditional—including divine authority: whatever is not fully trustworthy will cease to command full obedience. We are continually learning to judge more and more carefully what we can obey. To some religious people this use of our judgment is too great a liberty—and too harsh a disappointment in the long search for something we can trust uncritically. But anything worth trusting at all does not demand uncritical trust: it demands the growth of our conscience. The value of personal and poetic authority is that it teaches us judgment; conditional authority makes us establish conditions.

Of all the influences that have worked on me as I wrote the rituals, Jewish thought has been the strongest; in recent years it has come to be the measure of all my thinking. I am just beginning to sort out the widely varying attitudes toward authority in Jewish practice, but I find through all the variations an intense pursuit of conscience and an apparently inexhaustible urge toward careful judgment. I have not yet resolved what I think of the covenant as mandated by tradition, but I am profoundly convinced of the covenant written on the heart of which Jeremiah spoke—which one might take to be the matter-of-fact, unswerving faithfulness to the egalitarian, the skeptical, the practical and the wondrous all at once, that seems to surface wherever Jewish life has gone. I am left in the ironic position of accepting the authority of Judaism conditionally—because I trust it—and not because it is divine.

In essence, I have tried to devise a religious framework for people who have never been a religious community, whom no one has supposed to be the people of God, and to test it by certain principles of Jewish thought: that God is hidden and not to be named, that the development of character is a lifelong work of intellect and compassion, that critical thinking is an essential part of responsibility and that not even kindness is possible without it, and that any "absolute" short of this is a false comfort, an idol. If this nascent religion makes no claim to a covenant with God, it still presents an imperative: *If there is no covenant, we have to do it ourselves.*

E. M. Broner, whose work in Jewish feminist liturgy I admire, has said that ritual must incorporate both illusion and disillusion. I take this to mean both the sense of play or theater that makes it possible to enact one's great questions, and the sense of bone-seriousness that makes it possible to abandon sentimental pieties. I have thought for as long as I can remember that the asking of unanswerable questions and the facing of irreparable truths is our only consolation for having to live through them. The questions seem to become more unanswerable, and the truths more irreparable, all the time; but perhaps ritual can still provide a way of facing them together, and without despair.

Acknowledgments

Mark Doty, then at Goddard College, gave me much generous and intelligent commentary as the rituals were written. In the course of the manuscript's misadventures—of course it encountered incomprehension from many publishers—parts of it were published in periodicals: by Sy Safransky in *The Sun* (June/July 1992, reprinted in the anthology *Our Times/3*, ed. Robert Atwan [St. Martin's, 1993]), Kitty Axelson-Berry in the local weekly *The Valley Advocate* (October 7, 1993), and Joseph Cunneen and his colleagues in *Cross Currents* (Winter 1996/97). Donna Schaper kindly took notice of it in print several times. I am most grateful to my publisher, James K. Davies, for his interest in the book, and to Frederick T. Courtright for his expert and erudite handling of the permissions. Sarah Thomson was present at the book's conception, and her emotional integrity, intellectual acuity and domestic generosity upheld me during the writing as they have shaped my life.

Every effort has been made to identify copyright holders and obtain their permission to use quoted material. I am grateful to the authors and publishers for use of the following works:

Excerpt from "The Bed," from *Clearing* by Wendell Berry. Copyright © 1977 by Wendell Berry. Reprinted by permission of the author.

Excerpt from "The Chemical conviction" (J954) by Emily Dickinson. Reprinted by permission of the publishers and the Trustees of Amherst College from *The Poems of Emily Dickinson*, Thomas H. Johnson, ed., Cambridge, Mass.: The Belknap Press

Excerpt from "Mrs. Stein," by Alice Rabi Lichtenstein, from *Sojourner, The Women's Forum* (April 1986). Used by permission of the author.

Excerpt from "The School of Babylon," from *Selected Poems* by Thomas Blackburn. Copyright © 1975 by Thomas Blackburn. Reprinted by permission of Carcanet Press Ltd.

Excerpt from "Secrecy," from *The Ballad of the Outer Dark* by Vernon Watkins. Copyright © 1979 by Mrs Gwen Watkins. Used by permission of Mrs Gwen Watkins.

Excerpt from "Snow," from *China Trace* by Charles Wright (Wesleyan University Press, 1977). Copyright © 1977 by Charles Wright and reprinted by permission of Wesleyan University Press.

"Spell Against Sorrow," from *Collected Poems* by Kathleen Raine (Counterpoint, 2001). Copyright © 2001 by Kathleen Raine. Reprinted by permission of Counterpoint Press, a member of Perseus Books Group.

Excerpt from "Those Images," by W. B. Yeats. Reprinted with the permission of Scribner, an imprint of Simon & Schuster Adult Publishing Group, from *The Collected Works of W. B. Yeats, Volume I: The Poems*. Revised and edited by Richard J. Finneran. Copyright © 1940 by Georgie Yeats. All rights reserved. Also reprinted with the permission of A P Watt Ltd on behalf of Michael B. Yeats.

"Vita Amicae," from *Hard Words: And Other Poems* by Ursula K. LeGuin. Copyright © 1981 by Ursula K. LeGuin. Reprinted by permission of the author and the author's agents, the Virginia Kidd Agency, Inc.

Today then let us build a temple to the stars
we see above us now, burned out
ten million years ago; hosannahs
to the wind that shifts the silent dunes
without intent; and amen to the deep rot
of the forest floor, the subatomic world
we'll never see, the sweet collisions
and the million accidents of time
that gave us life—and all those miracles,
indifferent and inhuman as the waves
that Adam in his garden never dreamed
because they're no more kin
to him than heaven is to kings
or what is natural to what is named.

For what we love we can't call
names—what calls to us
in medias res, that thick green sedge
by the river, and we suppose it
as a bird, though what it is, is
singing.

—Eleanor Wilner

זה אלי ואנוהו

—Exodus 15:2

In Medias Res

Introduction

Prometheus Stealing Torah for the People:
Notes Toward New Liturgy

Liturgy is a bastard form, halfway between real life and literature. It is not the making of choices and the wearing of soul against soul in the unrehearsed and unrepeatable conditions of living; it is not the solitary study of the human condition in the world. It is an effort to shape ourselves and our future in each other's presence, to bind ourselves to doing what we ought to do, to hold each other to a moral vision that we honor. It is the *lyricism* of morality, not its action or its demonstration. It is an attempt to overcome the solitude of our choices—a solitude which descends on us again the moment we leave each other's presence, and which, if we did not have it, we would desperately desire.

Liturgical reform—which in our day tends to mean the translation of liturgies not only into the vernacular but out of the literary realm—is meant to make those liturgies accessible, but it merely makes them disappointing. Flat language insults both the intelligence and the ear; far from being a reprieve from a too-demanding literacy, it deprives both the literate and the illiterate of a viable oral tradition. Only if liturgy is capable of permeating the common language—as the Book of Common Prayer permeates English literature, as Hebrew permeates Yiddish—can it enter into people's thoughts. And only what enters our thoughts can alter our actions.

A liturgy without confidence suggests a God without confidence. Perhaps this is apt enough for the industrial age—which has surely given God one mortal blow after another—but the point of liturgy has never been to collapse under the weight of the status quo; it aims to change people. A liturgy that cannot change people conveys the message that the will and the spirit have no power, that we cannot do anything that really matters.

If the old liturgies are not possible to translate convincingly—if, to the translators, they are no longer effectual—perhaps it's because the conditions of life, the type and scope of the threats that face us, are new in human experience. We need liturgy to accomplish a new thing: not simply personal or collective communion with the holy, but the restoration—the re-creation—of the world.

Ritual is not a preliminary to living a good life, but a last-ditch attempt at healing (which the community repeats over and over at frequent intervals, hoping the hypnotic effect will enable it to "take").

To have serious poetry or religion you must first be convinced of the irreparable. The person who is searching for solutions, ways around private tragedy, is still undefeated and will find only superficial answers. New ideologies, popular psychologies, new friendships and love affairs, conversions, may be profoundly healing and invigorating, but they do not *solve* the former pain, any more than they prevent pain in the future. Old pain is still there, whole, unmanageable, whenever something touches it.

Tikkun—"repair"—arises only out of this recognition. Defeat is what teaches us the difference between the reparable and the irreparable. And defeat is what provides the impetus for repair: we find it unbearable that *even more* should be lost, and rush to prevent it.

Tikkun is not optimism, the cheerful faith that things can be repaired; it is the refusal to accept any more defeat.

Our business as spiritual beings is to outwit the inevitable.

A difficulty in the writing of liturgy is the division in our outward life between what is *understood* and what is *enacted*. What we know from reading books, and from living our lives, tends to be so much more complex and intimate than what we do in religious services; even when we recognize a passage or a thought we love in a service, if we are with people whose thoughts we don't know and to whom we can speak only with conventional kindliness and not with intensity, we may suspect we are reading something into the text. We get over expecting any direct relationship between participation and emotion.

Yet we want enactment. People want what they know to be sayable.

For some, religious services and spiritual paths may fail to touch religious feeling altogether. They do not encompass that complex of lights and sounds and smells that the world is to them between sleep and waking, or in our profoundest moments. For me there is a whole private realm—of moon and stars, intense cold, the smell of tanned skins and the howl of dogs, a certain silhouette of mountains, the shades of green from spruce to aspen—that is a lightning-rod from body to spirit; whatever I do for religion, no matter how deeply it touches me, there is always something elsewhere that is stronger.

The people for whom the lights and sounds and smells they encounter through religion *are* those primal things—for whom the sound of the shofar or the smell of incense or the taste of ritual wine become that lightning-rod—are they undivided?

Why are some people distressed at the thought of not having a "personal God"? Is it that they feel they would have to give up the biblical stories, which are so numinous and so endlessly complex? Is it simply the naïve form of belief they want, a God with nothing incalculable about him? Or do they mean that God moves them *in their person*—"in the inward parts"—and only the language of personality can hold that movement?

To rule out biblical metaphor as a means of talking about the world is like refusing to breathe air. It is polluted? Yes; but can you choose to be anaerobic instead?

Never mind the authority of the Bible. Does it move you to dream dreams and to see visions, and to think? To think about justice, even against its own pronouncements?

When the Bible is taken as a set of normative prescriptions that override common sense and individual judgment, *it prevents you from striving with God.*

If we accept the word "God" into our vocabulary, it is partly so we may have adequate curses. The mighty and disembodied must take its place beside the vulnerable and embodied—excrement and sex. Profanity is the metaphysical complement of obscenity; together they span the whole range of human reality.

To call God *he* or *she* and take part in the present wrangle over pronouns is servility. How can one pin a skirt or a codpiece on the immaterial? And to what purpose? Is God a "role model" that we should be able to emulate uncritically?

For the sake of the Hebrew Bible and liturgy—and of curses—I am willing, on the whole, to put up with *he*; this is a considered decision, made after years of feminist reading and living, and I do not take it as a defeat. Feminism has made it viscerally clear that the West's strongest image of the divine is a metaphor; to be aware of that all the time is one of the most powerful safeguards against spiritual complacency I know. (I wish I thought the metaphor of *she* as powerful a safeguard, but I don't; though it may dispel a certain amount of spiritual complacency among men, it forces on both men and women a self-conscious etiquette that is merely distracting, and encourages a wishful romanticism about God the Mother that is a far less interesting metaphor. God's biblical Fatherhood is at least convincing.) *He* is also a powerful confirmation, in specifically feminist terms, of an intuition that appears throughout the Bible in various ways: not that God is male and thus our rightful ruler, but that God is not entirely to be trusted.

Should we want to remove the paradox from worship?

Surely the epistemological difference between theism and atheism is not as great as either side supposes. The most convinced atheist must acknowledge that there are realms so different from one's conscious understanding that only religious metaphor will serve to identify them. The most convinced theist must acknowledge that religious metaphor always remains metaphor—that any name of God instantly becomes inadequate, reductive; that to say "God" and mean anything literal and limited by it is already to take the Name in vain.

Even if metaphor remains metaphor and the universe is "all there is," surely this is no threat to holiness. Surely the universe only confirms and ratifies that holiness is *there*, burning, inescapable, right down in the structure of our flesh, right in our atoms. *Adonai elohechem emet*—God is true, so true that our knowledge of that truth is bodily, God *cannot* abandon us; such abandonment is as inconceivable as that flesh should fly apart into loose molecules, or gravity cease to hold us down. Why should "materialism" seem opposed to supernaturalism, or immanence a threat to transcendence? Transcendence *is* immanent; holiness knits us together, bone to its bone. Immanence is transcendent; what we are *gives rise* to unrest and the dream of redemption. To take the terms "immanent" and "transcendent" as anything but groping attempts to express these realities is the most pedestrian literal-mindedness, unworthy even of theologians.

What is necessary is to remember holiness, not to define it. Holiness maintains us whether we remember it or not—for holiness is not some remote moral rectitude but every kindness that keeps us fed and warm and thinking and out of pain—but we may be too embittered or too unknowing to give it room. Holiness is inescapable, but an answering faithfulness to it is not inevitable. Neither the immanence nor the transcendence of God has ever been a guarantee of moral goodness.

Defenders of the immanent God (or Goddess) are accused of promoting self-indulgence, and they in turn accuse the defenders of the transcendent God of authoritarianism; there is some truth to both accusations, but only because each side insists on constructing itself in response to the other. If both sides paid attention to the content of experience (and, for that matter, of revelation), they might find the categories less definite.

There is something that loves you in the world. The voice that speaks to you within, in the worst despair, is not different from the voice that called the world into being. What makes your body give off heat is the same fire that sleeps in the rocks and is changed from light to matter by the plants: the fire that lights the sun and the other stars. To use Arthur Waskow's interpretation of a familiar formula, "Adonai" *is* "Elohenu"; the individual's "my Lord"—itself already a tongue-tied substitute for a name too like

the breath of life to be spoken—*is* the community's "our God."
The intimate *is* the infinite. To break that unity is to fall prey to
a series of barren and distracting arguments that try to rule the
whole of reality by a fragment of itself.

Are nature and history truly at odds as religious principles? Is
nature static and history dynamic, nature amoral and history the
realm of ethics? Only if one is naïve about either. Granting that it
is a good deal easier to be naïve about nature than history, we can
only maintain that romantic stance by seeing nature as untouched
by ourselves—a habit that becomes harder and harder to keep up
as the human population and its technology increase. We think
history stops and nature begins at the city limits, or just beyond the
guardrail; we neglect to hear "the voice of our brother's blood crying
out to us from the ground." No "scenery" is uninhabited; there is no
place on the planet that has not witnessed human conflict and human pain. "The dead are not under the earth," wrote Birago Diop:
"they are in the crying grass, they are in the moaning rocks." We go
to nature for peace; we love the trees because they are older than we
are, and discharge their responsibilities more gracefully. If we are
lucky, we can get so far as to meet the trees on their own terms: "an-
nihilating all that's made to a green thought in a green shade." But
nothing stays annihilated: smog creeps up the mountains, and the
permafrost melts, and refuse washes ashore, and there is no corner
of the earth that the dead have not entered. Can we meet them with
love and recognition, rather than guilt and dread?

Nature heals by covering scars; history probes the wound. Which
of these could we dispense with?

I remain agnostic on the question of the spiritual whereabouts
of the dead—resurrection, reincarnation, the transmigration of
souls. Two things seem true. In the simultaneity of time, every

personality that ever was exists forever; in the successiveness of time, the personality is coterminous with the body. Our practical experience of death knows no more than this, and it seems to me slighting to the distress of mourners to speculate on the details as if promoting some recycling scheme.

A spiritual quest tends to look like an endless insatiable search after "personal power" because that power ebbs the minute it is obtained. What effect does your private well-being have once you get to your job the next morning, to push the same papers or sell the same redundant and mostly unnecessary goods, participating helplessly in the world's wasting? You turn back, again and again, puzzled, for more "personal power" *because your political circumstances do not give it to you.*

Yet without that search, without that blind insistence on not merely doing your job but maintaining your ways before God, you lose compassion; you forget how to feel, either for yourself or for others. You read the paper and say, "Why all the fuss about people being disappeared? I, this moment, am disappeared, and *I* can take it."

The principled refusal of the Christian gospel, not because it is too demanding but because it makes the wrong demand. The doctrine that supernatural deliverance is all that can help us against our own sinful nature, and that this deliverance has somehow already been accomplished by the life of one person two thousand years ago; the preoccupation with personal salvation; the church's recurrent uneasiness with the intellect and the body, as though they implicitly challenged the whole scheme—all these seem to me a distraction from the pressing business of conducting ourselves justly toward each other and toward the world. The fact that some people who accept these doctrines are people of integrity seems to me to argue for a kind of "original goodness" that can persist in the face of heavy assaults, and not at all for the saving power of Christian belief against "original sin." What is holy in us, perhaps, is finally too strong and too sensible to be thrown off course by a theology, and can break forth in the most uncongenial of surroundings.

Our problem is to make the conditions of life worthy of what is holy. Each of us has some knowledge of the holy through experience (whether or not we have been taught one of its official revelations), and we liberate it or occlude it primarily through our actions. Certainly one may discover the holy through Christian practice and belief, and act according to Christian ethical principles; yet the further Christianity gets from its Hebrew origins, the more its idea of holiness is subtly altered. Holiness becomes dematerialized, taken out of time; it becomes remote from us, and we can only approach it by becoming remote from ourselves. Like a kind of antimatter, it is essentially irreconcilable with bodily life; the body of Christ (historical or sacramental) is the only place where flesh and holiness cohere. Some modern Christians deplore this flight from matter, and affirm the value of the body, but even this affirmation tends not to have the purposeful, unsanctimonious directness that the Jewish idea of holiness still preserves: a holiness that is not a kind of essence but a kind of activity. Holiness is warm, not cold.

It is not what the body *is* that matters—whether good or bad—but what it can become: what it can accomplish that is necessary to accomplish. Or, from the other side, the damage it can do, how it can lock the intimate away and keep it from the infinite.

The extreme beauty of Christian art and music and literature can break one's heart. Still, it cannot be allowed to submerge one's conscience.

Think of *Beowulf* and *Job* together: for all their differences, a certain similarity of tone. The severity, the vastness, the insistence that what really matters is maintaining one's ways—valor in the face of the universe, which is stronger than you are anyway. An affinity there that doesn't really exist between *Beowulf* and the Gospels. The Anglo-Saxons didn't need to be saved; they would have taken to Judaism undiluted.

A Judeo-Pagan tradition?

If we do not hope for supernatural deliverance, perhaps we hope in bodily life itself: in the body's mysterious, self-renewing capacity for living, in the mind's elusive, self-preserving trick of withdrawing from assault; in the fact of being alive, which we cannot trace to its molecular source, but which endows us even so with a kind of autonomic wisdom.

Philip Rawson (in *Primitive Erotic Art*) puts the effort to understand this aliveness in the form of an equation, which may occur to us when a beloved person dies:

$$\text{This dead body} = \text{the live body I know, minus X}$$
$$X = \text{the live body minus the dead body}$$

Hope is, or proceeds from, X: from the thing that ceases to animate the body when death comes, but until then operates with an extraordinary tenacity, a dauntlessness almost as horrifying as it is reassuring. It operates in the brutalized as in the lucky, in the severely ill as in the healthy, in the child hated by its parents, the inmate in the camp, the patient who survives as a body without a mind. The body gives up being alive only with great difficulty. "I will set my covenant in your flesh," said God to Abraham—speaking of that least autonomic bodily process, circumcision—but the involuntary processes are the root and proof of the covenant. The body says (or "X" in the body says, or God in the form of "X" says), *I will be the covenant in your flesh. I will not let you off easy. I will hold you to life.*

The tiresomeness, the frivolity, the sheer redundancy of people when you see them anonymously (does the world need so many of them? does the world need *you?*)—and the preciousness, the heartbreaking uniqueness, the admirable resiliency of the ones you know!

Liturgy is about that resiliency, the reasonless, bodily, flat-out *here I am* of being here: being here and being glad. *L'chaim.*

Jacob Neusner's idea of liturgy as "enchantment," an act of imagination that transforms the *is* of ordinary life into the *as if* of community and holiness. The world grows more "disenchanted" all the time: there is palpably less and less community, and arguably less and less holiness, in it. On what basis can we enchant the world, and when is such enchantment not a fraudulent, romantic effort to see ourselves as more important than we are, to cling to the illusion that the universe loves us best? When is enchantment a form of valor, of *tikkun?*

Imagine a seasonal ritual as an enchantment that does not depend on what the universe thinks of the community but on what the community thinks of the universe. We invest the earth's activity with moral meaning, we try to assist it, we imagine ourselves not as important but as obligated. Liturgy makes deliberate the involuntary: we participate consciously in what the world does "by nature." Not the "pathetic fallacy" whereby we imagine the world feels as we do, but the ritual enactment whereby we feel as it does.

Simultaneously, we enchant morality with the grace of what the earth does. Too much of what we understand as morality is bleak and harsh: mere prohibition without wonder or sweetness or reward—say, the commandment against idols, which deprives, without the commandment to keep the Sabbath, which restores. But if morality is not beautiful—if it is seen primarily as a check on beauty, a limitation on the aesthetic sense itself—who will be able to bear its pursuit?

Morality and grace need each other: both the intentional and the habitual, both the decisive and the beautiful. If morality is only the idol-smasher, it becomes cruel, and then it loses its power; idol-smashing burns itself out, and returns to idolatry, because peace must come from somewhere. But if morality is enchanted, it becomes not merely a destructive force, reducing everything to the irredeemable rubble of what is: it becomes a reminder of, a passport to, what can be.

Notes on the Form and Performance of the Rituals

I have organized the cycle on the lines of an obvious and indisputable cosmology—the solar calendar—and a system which is outdated as chemistry but fully alive as metaphor, the four elements. This is fairly standard practice in neopagan circles, where I first encountered it as a liturgical structure, but I am taking it in a direction I have not seen there. Whereas the eight solar holidays (the solstices, the equinoxes and the midpoints between them) are usually regarded as cyclical celebrations, evidence of the reliability of nature, I have tried to recognize that the reliability of nature is now profoundly in question, and that the trustworthiness of human civilization has been more thoroughly undermined in our own times than at any time before. To approach civilization without reference to these life-disrupting facts—as if the ozone were still intact, as if the Bomb had never fallen, as if the Jews of Europe had not died—is not only to ignore the dead and the endangered, but to underestimate the impulse to celebration itself, as if it could only exist in a closed garden, a safe and artificial place.

I have also followed standard practice in assigning the roles of the four elements to the persons who stand at the four cardinal points in the circle of participants. (Earth stands at the north, Air at the east, Fire at the south, Water at the west. Occasionally they do not speak in this order, and it should be noted that the order *Earth, Water, Air, Fire* represents the ascent through the four kabbalistic "worlds" of action, emotion, intellect and the ineffable.) But I have made room for a fifth element which is not generally given a role in neopagan ritual, though it is part of the same Aristotelian cosmology. It is sometimes called spirit, or aether, or essence, in contrast to the materiality of the other elements; I have chosen its most cryptic name, the Quintessence ("fifth element"), because the other terms lend themselves to a spirituality so ethereal that it tends to float away from the particulars of life. What I mean by the Quintessence is something close to Robertson Davies' "Fifth Business"; the force that makes things happen, the thing that animates the inanimate, the fact of relationship itself that emerges from the space between. In theological terms it is something like Harold Schulweis' "predicate theology": God is not a person but a motive power, the transforming event in all the stages (say) of photosynthesis and harvesting and kneading and baking involved in "bringing forth bread from the earth." No person and no thing can *represent* this power—not because it is forbidden but because it is impossible—but words can remind; it seemed useful to let it have a voice among the others. I suggest that the role be rotated among the members of any group using the rituals; to have the same person read it every time, as if transformation were not always in transit, would be misleading.

In the series of rituals for life passages I have not tried to encompass the whole range of what is possible or necessary, but to do what I had some instinct for and let it suggest a pattern for further work. I have tried to keep a particular balance between the personal and the communal: to suggest that we are linked and responsible for each other, but that the validity of our linkage depends on our regard for each other's solitude—a generous mutual detachment in which each person has serious work and free choice, as much as the world allows.

I have said as clearly as I could in the rituals, but perhaps it bears saying in cold prose, that I have no ultimate answers. If I acknowledge only personal and poetic authority in others, the last thing I want is to set myself up as an institutional authority. I am not in the business of getting people to leave their nets and follow me. I am pleased whenever people use these rituals, but I would be rather alarmed if anyone began using them exclusively, or tried to base some thoroughgoing system on them. "When I tell a truth," said Blake, "it is not to convince those who do not know it but to protect those who do." I do not want my work used as dogma when it is really a sort of philosophical drama. Of course I hope it will have moral consequences, but *belief* would be beside the point. Thus I also think it would be beside the point for members of institutional religions to view me with alarm; I am not in competition with them. (I am, from time to time, critical of institutional religions—and particularly of Christianity, for which I harbor a disappointed love of thirty years' standing—but I do not expect them to evaporate under my criticism.) In the end there must be room for both institutional and personal authority—for orthodoxy and heresy—because there are people who need each one. And perhaps each one shades into the other where it least expects to, so that finally a certain ironic generosity is required from both sides.

Seasonal Rituals

Invocations

In neopagan practice, a ritual is generally bracketed by the calling and dismissal of the elements. Names of gods and goddesses are often attached to them—not always with any decisively theistic intention—but I am less interested in such personifications than in our common experience. Following from John Cowper Powys' notion of "Elementalism" (as detailed in *A Philosophy of Solitude* [New York: Simon & Schuster, 1933]), I have presented the elements as inanimate, except for the Quintessence which plays by its own rules.

I offer three alternatives here for the openings of the seasonal rituals. (They are to be used for all but the Feast of Fools, which contains its own parodic invocations.) Version I is essentially a philosophical statement; version II is shorter and more lyrical than philosophical; version III is lighter and more celebratory.

I

Quintessence:

We stand, random and unchosen, in this circle. Not the people who were called, but the people who gathered; not the people who were taught, but the people who sought to know; not the people of faith, but the people who would be faithful.

All:

All we were given is broken: the light of religion, the honor of the past, the extent of the future, the health of the world. Neither faith nor reason can rise to this occasion; only compassion, the tender ordering of re-lations, can take these fragments and make of them some worthy thing. Through that work of mending let memory be honored, let justice be nurtured, let humanity at last become humane.

Quintessence:

We mark here the sun's turning of a corner in time; let us bless the elements of making.

Earth:

Bless the earth, the foundation: keeper of deeds, to which our lives are the compost; loam of the womb and stone of the grave, the barren and the garden, the rock that upholds us and the tremor at its heart; without which we are not.

All:

We bless the earth, and give gratitude for matter.

Water:

Bless the water, the mover: keeper of feeling, which dissolves and returns to us all that we cast away; the rain and the river, the well and the wave, marsh and tide, mist and ice; without which we are not.

All:

We bless the water, and give thanks for what flows.

Air:

Bless the air, the world's breath: keeper of intellect, quickener of thought, whisper of symbiosis between us and the trees; without which we are not.

All:

We bless the air, and rejoice in what rises.

Fire:

Bless the fire, the igniter: keeper of vision, which illumines by raging and warms by consuming; of all tools the most ambiguous, at once sustaining and deadly; spark and furnace, hearth and star, finite and insatiable; without which we are not.

All:

We bless the fire, and tremble at its burning.

Quintessence:

Bless the midst, the unnameable: that which is called love by some and chaos by others, and is the power of relation; which grows wild in the intervals and in the spaces between; which unmakes and recombines; which whispers the word of division in our cells, and unites all things in one embrace; by which we are made, by which we are broken, and without which we are not.

All:

Call us to return home, heart of our homelessness, eye of our weeping; distance between the *is* and the *ought,* we will travel you.

II

Earth:

And the world said: I am old, and you have dug me
and builded me and poured out your poisons on me;
but I am not dead, and I hold you.

Air:

And the wind said, I carry: the seed and the feather,
the rain and the thunder, the ash of your engines, the
dust of your dead, and I weary; but I am your breath,
and I quicken you.

Fire:

And the flame said: why will you drive me? You who
should love me bind me in slavery. I never weary, but
I serve no one, and I will not serve you.

Water:

And the waves said, shallow; while you live I will fill
you; clean or unclean, I hallow; but I ran here before
you, and I will follow.

Quintessence:

And the unnameable said: where are you? Will you
not speak when I call you? I draw life from the stones
and the water; I teach the flesh to grow warm and the
leaf to flutter. When will you do what I teach, and not
what destroys you? I will not be summoned, but I will
be present among you.

III

Earth:

Let earth rejoice with the shoreline.

Water:

For boundaries are the proof of the strong.

Air:

Let air rejoice with the trees.

Earth:

For rootedness plays in the fields of heaven.

Fire:

Let fire rejoice with the darkness.

Air:

For ferocity is the measure of yearning.

Water:

Let water rejoice with the sun.

Fire:

For dazzle is the garment of clarity.

Quintessence:

And let rejoice among them that limitless, that everywhere unrooted, that fierce and glittering one from which all powers derive: matrix of galaxies, force of interstices, law of relation.

Conclusion

To be read at the end of all the seasonal rituals except the Feast of Fools.

Quintessence:

> The ritual is ended. We thank time and space for holding us here, and we bless the elements of making:

Earth:

> Earth, which is the gravity of love;

Air:

> Air, which is the levity of love;

Fire:

> Fire, which is the passion of love;

Water:

> Water, which is the patience of love;

Quintessence:

> And the presence of the Absence, which is love itself among them: remote beyond conceiving, intimate beyond mistaking, unto whom all that draws breath gives praise.

Winter Solstice

The seasonal rituals are made for the northern hemisphere, and for a certain narrow zone even of that. There is no use in apologizing; the imagination cannot respond to every latitude at once, or respond lovingly and accurately to climates it has not experienced. In effect this is a safeguard against false universalism on the writer's part and passivity on the reader's. When experience jars with the text, the reader can write a new text. Even religions that claim to be universal have their geographies, having started somewhere; their far-flung proselytes find ways of adapting the originating experience to their own.

To be held after sunset. Enough candles are needed to distribute to each participant at a later point in the ritual, with some sort of shield to catch drips. Before the ritual begins, the double circle for the candle lighting should be rehearsed, so those who are stepping in to make the inner circle know who they are and everyone knows which direction to walk through the circle.

*The room is in darkness, except for five candles held by the **Elements**.*

Choose one of the Invocations, pp. 20–24.

*__Elements__ (or one singer with **All** holding a drone note):*

> The world is old tonight, the world is old
> the stars above the fold do show their light
> do show their light
> and so they did and so
> a thousand years ago
> and so will do my friends when we lie cold

The world is still tonight, the world is still
the snow upon the hill like wool lies white
    like wool lies white
and so it did and so
a thousand years ago
and so will do my love
when we like will

Earth:

The sun has withdrawn and left us to the night.
Winter is harsh for the warm creatures: we shrink
from the cold and hide ourselves from the wind. Our
life is an effort to avert all that threatens; we get our
strength from resistance. Winter is the threat of the
irresistible.

As the next song is sung, the **Quintessence** *walks around the circle
blowing the candles out.*

Elements:

The day is past and gone,
The evening shades appear;
O may we all remember well
The night of death is near.

We lay our garments by
Upon our beds to rest;
So death will soon disrobe us all
Of what we here possess.

And when our days are past,
And we from time remove,
O may we in thy bosom rest,
The bosom of thy love.

Water:

> What do you hide from the wind's howling? What is your holy secret?

Air:

> What seed do you carry, coiled in dormancy, into the bitter night?

Fire:

> Shelter it well: that is the fire that will warm you, and turn the great wheel over. Not that the world needs us to turn its face toward summer, but that the world holds us in the darkness, and kindles the will to strike light.

Silence is kept for a time.

Earth:

> Crumbs of rotten stone,
> shards of bone, the leavings
> and the ruins of lives—
> the ground's a grave, and so
> it thrives. Another day,
> another day, sing
> the sleepers in their bed.
> Under the bitter ice,
> among the overthrown are hid
> the seeds, in whose dark
> the future and the past
> internested lie,
> two lovers in their sleep.
> A thousand thousand years
> will bloom here in the spring,
> upon the living sing
> the blessing of the dead.

Elements:

> We are awake in the night!
> We turn the wheel to bring the light!
> We call the sun from the womb of night!

When the chant has been sung the first time, **Fire** *lights a candle. As the chanting continues, every other person in the circle steps inward so that two concentric circles are formed. The people in the two circles face each other and join hands overhead to make a circular tunnel. One by one, starting with the person on* **Fire's** *left, each person goes through the tunnel walking toward the left (clockwise).* **Fire** *hands each one a lighted candle as they pass. As the people return to their places with the candles, the circle will slowly light up. The chanting continues till everyone has gone through.*

The Conclusion (p. 25) is read.

Notes

The world is old... "Shepherd's Carol," traditional. Recorded
by Jean Ritchie, *Kentucky Christmas* (Greenhays GR 717). I
have slightly altered the words in two places.

The day is past and gone... John Leland, "Evening Shade" (1835).
Several musical settings exist; I was listening to the one on
*Rivers of Delight: American Folk Hymns from the Sacred Harp
Tradition* by Word of Mouth Chorus (Nonesuch H-71360).
The written music may be found in *Original Sacred Harp:
Denson Revisions 1971: Standard Melodies* (Bremen, Georgia:
Sacred Harp Publishing Co., 1971).

Crumbs of rotten stone... Wendell Berry, "The Bed," in *Clearing*
(New York: Harcourt Brace Jovanovich, 1977), 37.

We are awake in the night... Starhawk, *The Spiral Dance* (San
Francisco: Harper & Row, 1979), 172.

The Trees' Praise

It is not misanthropic to recognize that we have disrupted our surroundings irrecoverably and with results that we can only guess at in their general outlines. It is not lugubrious and self-flagellating to mourn this chain of events and to fear the future. Nonetheless we generally hold it a psychological necessity and in a sense a moral duty to avoid paralyzing guilt. The tragedy of being ethical animals is that we are still animals: our life drives us to keep on living, to maintain our loves and our work, to see what happens next. We have conflicting duties: obligations to the planet and to the long term, which might be better off without us, but also obligations in the short term to our families and communities, whom we cannot abandon.

I do not believe in forgiveness; guilt is a fact of life, and one goes on from it. Even rituals that undertake to forgive our sins cannot arrest their consequences. Rituals of forgiveness, unless they are mere wishful thinking, are compressed enactments of a complex process of active reparation and gradual forgetfulness which slowly turns unbearable conditions to bearable ones; they give us an escape not from the guilt but from the paralysis. With or without forgiveness, ritual is a way of not abandoning hope—that is (in Dante's terms) of not being in hell.

To be held in the daytime, at the midpoint between the winter solstice and the spring equinox (roughly February 2). If weather permits, the ritual may take place in the woods or in a garden; otherwise in a shelter with woods or garden close by. In the center of the circle are garlands of fruit and nuts, cakes of suet and birdseed, and other ornaments for the trees.

Choose one of the Invocations, pp. 20–24.

Quintessence:

> I shall celebrate the season, and carry the salvation of roots to distant parts.

Earth:

> We honor the trees, keepers of quiet, whose branches rise in the heights, and whose roots sink in the dark among rock and trickle. We honor the strong bones of their winter sleep.

Air:

> We honor the green hush of their lavish summer.

Fire:

> Our life emerges from the life of trees: our shelter from their shade, their wood in our houses, our words on their paper, their breath in our lungs. We renew the air for each other: what one scatters the other gathers, and life continues in balance.

Water:

> Can we restore the balance? We have overburdened the air. We fill it with smoke, we dissolve the ozone above it, we alter its chemistry. We have broken the covenant of breath, the one demonstrable speech between us and the green things.

Earth:

> How long will the trees keep the covenant of breath?
> We unbury their ancestors, the ancients mummi-
> fied to coal and oil. We burn them for fuel, and their
> ghosts hover above us.

Air:

> Mystery of carbon, that turns from air to matter and
> back again.

Fire:

> Mystery of entropy, the solid turned to smoke, dis-
> persed and lost.

Water:

> Who shall gather the smoke of the dead wood
>   burning,
> Or behold the flowing years from the sea returning?

*At this point the **Elements** begin to speak in reverse order.*

Fire:

> The smoke hangs in the heavens.

Air:

> It enters the rain.

Earth:

> The parched eviscerate soil
> Gapes at the vanity of toil,
> Laughs without mirth.
>   This is the death of earth.

All:

> Under the sun's eye all is exposed to mutation. The
> spell of our creation is read backward.

Quintessence:

> Nature's polluted,
> There's man in every secret corner of her,
> Doing damned wicked deeds. Thou art old, world,
> A hoary atheistic murderous star;
> I wish that thou would'st die, or could'st be slain.

Silence. Slowly the **Elements,** *and then* **All,** *begin to sing low, flat
moaning notes. When this mourning has spent itself the* **Elements** *begin a wordless chant with a calm, sustaining tune. When the others
have joined in and a sense of stability has been re-established,* **All,** *still
singing, take fruit and birdseed and other ornaments and hang them on
the trees. Then they return to the circle.*

Water:

> For there is hope for a tree, if it be cut down, that
> it will sprout again, and its tender branch not cease.
> Though the root grow old in the ground, and the
> stump die in the earth, it will bud at the scent of wa-
> ter and put forth shoots like a plant.

Air:

> Not by might, not by power, but by breath. Hope is
> simple persistence: the slow indrawing and release of
> breath, the drawing down of spirit into deed. One cell
> at a time, chlorophyll conducts the air's conversion.
> One act at a time, we begin the air's restoration.

All:

> Through our persistence let the green tree spring from the dry, and the tree of knowledge restore the tree of life.

Quintessence:

> How does the tree's crown turn light into green?

All:

> Through gratitude: so it discovers and does the law of its being.

Quintessence:

> How does that light descend into the branches?

All:

> Through understanding, that knows its work without having learned it; and through wisdom, that learns and does what it did not know.

Quintessence:

> How does the tree maintain its symmetry?

All:

> Through severity, that makes no more than is necessary; and through mercy, whereby the necessary is made sufficient.

Quintessence:

> How do the branches join to the bole?

All:

Through beauty, which governs all joinings.

Quintessence:

How does the tree's wood stand against the weather?

All:

Through authority, which allows it to ascend; and through endurance, which allows it to bend.

Quintessence:

How does it enter the earth?

All:

Through desire, which longs to be rooted.

Quintessence:

In what kingdom are those roots secured?

All:

In the kingdom of matter, where all that lives is grounded and sheltered.

Quintessence:

Earth! What is it you urgently ask for if not transformation?

All:

Earth, my love, I will do it.

Quintessence:

> For the burden of matter is the indrawn breath of a
> word that may change all.

The Conclusion (p. 25) is read.

Notes

I shall celebrate the season… Edmond Jabès, *El, or the Last Book. The Book of Questions*, v. 7, trans. Rosmarie Waldrop (Middletown, CT: Wesleyan University Press, 1984), 46.

Who shall gather the smoke… J. R. R. Tolkien, *The Two Towers. The Lord of the Rings*, v. 2 (Boston: Houghton Mifflin, 1954), 112.

The parched eviscerate soil… T. S. Eliot, "Little Gidding," in *Four Quartets. The Complete Poems and Plays*, 1909-1950 (New York: Harcourt, Brace and Company, 1952), 140.

The spell of my creation is read backward. Thomas Lovell Beddoes, *Death's Jest-Book*, act 4, scene 3.

Nature's polluted… ibid., act 2, scene 3 (var.)

For there is hope for a tree… Job 14:7-9 (a mix of several translations).

Not by might, not by power, but by breath. Zech. 4:6.

The questions and answers about the life of trees are loosely based on the Kabbalistic diagram of the Tree of Life, composed of ten *sefirot* or emanations of divinity.

Earth!…I will do it. Rainer Maria Rilke, Ninth Duino Elegy, in *Duino Elegies*, trans. David Young (New York: Norton, 1978), 83.

For the burden of matter… John Cowper Powys, *A Philosophy of Solitude* (New York: Simon and Schuster, 1933), 233.

The Feast of Fools

The Feast of Fools was a tradition in the medieval church; sufficient record of it remains that early music performers have discovered and recorded parodic Masses written for such occasions. The holiday was blasphemous, silly, scatological, a chance to let out all the low puns that occurred to pious people during the year (e.g., *ornemus*—"let us gamble"—for *oremus*, "let us pray"), and to mock the clergy who were owed such deference the rest of the time. In Judaism a comparable tradition survives in Purim (without the blasphemy, but then it is scarcely necessary to blaspheme a God who established Jewish existence on such precarious grounds and who is at once *revelatus* and *absconditus*). Many other traditions contain a holiday based on the reversal of norms. This version has come out as a blasphemy against Christian norms, partly because of the medieval tradition and partly because Christianity is the chief religion in the West to have set itself up as normative, but I have let Christianity off fairly easy and fairly affectionately; I could, like the medievals, have satirized the Mass. Others are invited to adapt the ritual to their own preferences and targets, with the caveat that topical political humor is likely to be tedious if it merely reiterates standard positions.

*To be held on either the spring equinox or April Fool's Day. The ritual should be well rehearsed by the **Elements** and performed without books. The people gather in procession near the place where the ritual will be performed. A singer representing the **Quintessence** leads the procession, and the other **Elements** end it. Before the procession begins to move, a song is sung.*

Quintessence:

> The light of day
> is joy's light today,
> I judge. With sadness
>
> whoever grieves
> let them be relieved
> by this solemn madness.
>
> And on this day
> down with the narrow way,
> down with envy and malice.
>
> Let all who will
> laugh their silly fill
> at the feast of the ass.

*The procession begins to move, singing the song that follows. The **Elements** at the end are accompanied by a pantomime donkey with two people in it who produce noises (braying, duck calls, etc.) at the "Hey! hey! hey!" of the chorus. The procession advances into the ritual space and forms a circle, the donkey perhaps balking or wandering off and the **Elements** whacking it along. The donkey is finally taken into the circle.*

Elements:

> Water, water is my state,
> Air my inspiration,
> Fire is my igniting place,
> Earth my destination.
>   *Hey! hey! hey! Let us bray!*
>
> Ego, Id and Super-E-
> Go to fill our need, O!
> Three in one and one in three,
> Subject to libido.
>   *Hey! hey! hey! Let us bray!*

> We are made of mortal stuff,
> Dust and ashes merely,
> Like a leaf the wind can toss
> Down the sidewalk serely.
> *Hey! hey! hey! Let us bray!*

The donkey, upon finding itself alone in the circle, carries on a conversation in comic noises between its two ends. Eventually, in this attempt to communicate, it becomes entangled in its costume, throws it off, and the two people within stand revealed as **Pan** *and* **Gaea**.

Pan:

Mother!

Gaea:

Son!

They strike a tableau of Michelangelo's most familiar Pietà.

Gaea (consulting her watch after a short time):

Pan, you lazy boy, get up! It's spring, and you *know* what that means. Rise and shine! Up and at 'em! (*She jolts him a bit on her knee and he springs up.*)

Pan (bewildered):

Up and Adam? I thought it was Adam and Eve. (*Exasperated,* **Gaea** *walks away from him.*) Adam and Steve?

Gaea:

Fool!

Pan:

> If the fool would persist in his folly he would become wise.

*Pan goes to the circumference of the circle, pulls **Earth** into the center, and spins him or her dizzily around.*

Pan:

> Some speak of a return to nature.

Earth:

> I wonder where they could have been.

*Pan returns **Earth** to **Fire**'s place, just as **Gaea** pulls **Fire** into the center. They repeat this pattern, pulling the **Elements** one by one out of their places in the circle, whirling them around and returning them to the wrong places, and causing general commotion. As this goes on, they all shout out proverbs.*

Gaea (to Fire):

> Don't cuss the climate. It probably doesn't like you any better than you like it.

Air (to Pan):

> The wages of sin is death!

Pan:

> But the hours are good!

Gaea (to Water):

> The hours of folly are measured by the clock.

Water:

> But of wisdom no clock can measure.

Fire (to Pan):

> What is life?

Pan:

> One damned thing after another!

Earth (to Gaea):

> I suppose the human race is doing the best it can—

Gaea:

> — but hell's bells, that's only an explanation, it's not an excuse.

Pan (to Water):

> Do not ask for whom the bell tolls. Just answer it.

Air (to Gaea):

> But there is very little justice in the universe!

Gaea:

> What is the use of being the universe if you have to be just? (*She looks around, outraged.* **Pan** *crouches to avoid her wrath.*)
> We have wasted paradox and mystery on you, when all you ask us for is cause and effect!

An awful silence.

Pan (after a moment, helpfully):

> I got one. What's sticky and white and falls from the sky? (*He waits; no one responds.*) Kingdom Come!

The Elements rush out of their places and encircle him and Gaea, making an angry clamor that culminates in:

Elements:

> Is nothing sacred?

Pan:

> Is anything profane?

He leaps lightly out from between them and dances around them. Then he turns each Element outward with a kiss to face the larger circle, and each one speaks:

Earth:

> Theology says: "Reverence God or perish."

Air:

> Morality says: "Reverence Sex or perish."

Fire:

> Nationalism says: "Reverence the State or perish."

Water:

> And the poet and the clown reply:

Elements, Pan and Gaea:

> "We reverence Nature, and are prepared to perish."

*The **Elements** begin to hum a tune. Along with **Pan** and **Gaea**, they return to the circle and draw the people into a dance, weaving in and out among them and taking hands as they go. When **All** have joined hands, the **Elements** begin to sing the recessional—to the tune of "Jesus Christ is Risen Today"—and lead everyone away.)*

Elements:

> Pan the Fool is up today: Io Evohe!
> May he flourish every day: Io Evohe!
> Who did once beneath the frost: Io Evohe!
> Make believe that he was lost: Io Evohe!
>
> Now set free from narrow straits: Io Evohe!
> Wander back through Eden's gates: Io Evohe!
> Malt does more than Milton can: Io Evohe!
> To justify God's ways to man: Io Evohe!

Notes

The light of day... My translation of *"Lux hodie,"* from a twelfth-century Feast of Fools ceremony. The tune for this, and for "Water, water is my state" which follows *("Orientis partibus"),* can be heard on The Boston Camerata, *A Medieval Christmas* (Elektra/Nonesuch 971315–2).

We are made of mortal stuff... My translation of a verse of *"Estuans interius,"* from the *Carmina Burana* collection: *Factus de materia/cinis elementi/similis sum folio/de quo ludunt venti.* The song can be heard in full on any recording of Carl Orff's *Carmina Burana* (though his tune is too bitter for the occasion).

If the fool... would become wise. William Blake, *The Marriage of Heaven and Hell.*

Some speak...could have been. Frederick Sommer, *Venus, Jupiter & Mars: The Photographs of Frederick Sommer,* ed. John Weiss (Wilmington: Delaware Art Museum, 1980), 19.

Don't cuss...than you like it. Don Marquis, "certain maxims of archy," in *archy and mehitabel* (Garden City: Doubleday, 1930), 55.

The wages...hours are good. Not sure where I first heard this.

The hours of folly...can measure. Blake, *Marriage.*

What is life?...after another. Duncan Phillips, *The Enchantment of Art* (New York: John Lane Co., 1914), 25.

I suppose...not an excuse. Don Marquis, "archy says," in *the lives and times of archy and mehitabel* (Garden City: Doubleday, 1950), 407.

Do not ask...just answer it. From the horoscope column of the San Francisco Examiner on some forgotten date in the late 1980s.

But there is...have to be just? Don Marquis, "unjust," in *archy and mehitabel,* 156.

We have wasted…cause and effect! Christopher Fry, *The Lady's Not for Burning* (New York: Oxford University Press, 1950), 53.

What's sticky…Kingdom Come. Heard through the clerical grapevine at Michigan State University Library in the mid-1980s.

Theology says…and are prepared to perish. John Cowper Powys, *Rabelais* (New York: Philosophical Library, 1951), 378.

The hymn "Jesus Christ Is Risen Today" can be found in any Anglican / Episcopal hymnal, and in some other Protestant hymnals.

Narrow straits. A nod to Passover; the deliverance from Egypt is, in Hebrew, the deliverance from Mitzrayim, which translates "narrow straits."

Malt does more…God's ways to man. A. E. Housman, "Terence, This is Stupid Stuff," in *A Shropshire Lad.*

Mayday

The coming of full spring has given rise to the most contradictory ritual responses. There are pagan, Christian and communist Maydays; the month has been dedicated to courtship and to the Virgin Mary; there is a superabundance of meaning and little to tie the various meanings together. For that reason, this ritual has been rewritten several times. The present version brings in photosynthesis (including the curious fact that leaves are green because they absorb red light); metabolism, and the release of stored energy into kinetic energy; superabundance and waste, biodegradable and nonbiodegradable; and the human quirk of loving our own handiwork once it becomes "antique." The material on made objects evolved from Elaine Scarry's discussion in *The Body in Pain* of the early Marx, especially the idea of commodities as "congealed labor."

Partly as a caution against the utopian—the religious ardor that would impose wholesale chastity or compulsory motherhood, the ideological ardor that would glorify the most soulless labor, the ecological ardor (distinguished from desperation by its self-pride) that would shame us for breathing, cooking our food, or throwing anything away—this ritual shows us as somewhat stubbornly imperfectible. There is an element of Bosch's *Garden of Earthly Delights* at work in it: the innocent wreckage of those absorbed in physical life, their activities grotesque and inexplicable to observers but wholly necessary to themselves. Freud's "love and work"—the aims and the fruits of psychological health—make us free of the human realm, but do not set us above it; once free to act, we still act like human animals.

Each person brings to the ritual some object of human manufacture—old or new, beautiful or ugly, beloved or despised. When the circle is formed, the objects are put in the center.

Choose one of the Invocations, pp. 20–24. The third version may be especially useful here.

Fire:

> This is fire's season. The light increases, and the green things devour it; red plunges into the heart of the cell, consumed into its contrary, and the leaves unfold.

Air:

> Air, rocks and water all burn in secret, their light locked and unseen. But living things are flame.

All:

> The green things eat the sun, and we eat the green things; their stored sunlight powers us to move and work. At the solar plexus our food is disassembled, and we ignite: we are so many stars, reflecting the burning of our star.

Water:

> Energy is eternal delight.

Earth:

> What is Spring? –
> Growth in every thing –
> Flesh and fleece, fur and feather,
> Grass and greenworld all together.

All:

> Superabundant, prodigal, we take our place among
> them.

Quintessence:

> All that lives and breeds makes much too much. Apple
> blossoms, maple seeds, fish eggs, mosquitoes, kittens:
> the sheer exuberant waste of living things. Earth,
> air and water are infested with tangles and swarms
> and schools of living flame. We too make much too
> much: the middens, the ruins, the refuse and residue
> of our forbears prefigure our own continents of trash.
> We can no more live without waste than milkweeds
> can make one seed or mosquitoes one egg.

All:

> Exuberance is beauty. We make more than enough so
> that some of it will be enough. Let the sun's light see
> and bless even our waste.

*Each **Element** in turn comes to the center of the circle and picks up one
of the objects.*

Earth:

> How the object becomes subject when it enters a hu-
> man dwelling; how the inanimate tool, made without
> love, absorbs the life of feeling. First it is inert: labor
> frozen into matter, stricken with terror or remorse.
> At last through use that frozen posture softens, and it
> takes on the first grace of being taken for granted.

Water:

> As a person who is loved returns love, so an object that is saved reflects the feeling turned on it. Then the quantity of life given up to its making stands present, sad and beloved. Then our light starts forth from it, radiant and plain.

Quintessence:

> There are weavers who make one error in the pattern of a rug, to let their spirits out. There are sculptors who work in ice, letting their art melt with the day's passing. There are lovers whose work is to constellate taste and touch and sound and scent in atmospheres of grace that vanish with the morning. All things become precious through the damages of time.

Air:

> When we are dust, our possessions will be loved as substitutes for our dust.

Fire:

> While we are flame, let us burn. Love and work: make more, make more.

All:

> Eternity is in love with the productions of time.

Quintessence:

> The growing light reveals us, increases us, convicts us of the crime of our existence.

All:

> But where the crime's committed
> The crime can be forgot.

Quintessence:

> Reasonless, purposeful, resolute: bless, bless!

All:

> Reasonless, purposeful, resolute: bless, bless!

Maypole dance, tying the objects to the ends of the ribbons.

All (singing):

> Merrily, merrily shall I live now
> Under the blossom that hangs on the bough.

The Conclusion (p. 25) is read, and the people recover their possessions— or trade them—and take them home.

Notes

Energy is eternal delight. William Blake, *The Marriage of Heaven and Hell.*

What is Spring? Gerard Manley Hopkins, "May Magnificat."

Exuberance is beauty. Blake, *Marriage.*

Eternity is in love with the productions of time. Blake, *Marriage.*

But where the crime's committed... W. B. Yeats, "A Woman Young and Old."

Reasonless, purposeful, resolute... An impressionistic response to the *Barekhu*, the call to prayer in Jewish services, with its circular formula, "Bless the Lord who is blessed."

Merrily, merrily... William Shakespeare, *The Tempest*, 5.1.93–94.

Midsummer

Like "Mayday," this ritual has been entirely re-written; the first version seemed to me even at the time of writing inadequate and callow. This version is more frightening—not as frightening as the full Deuteronomic catalogue of curses, from which I have omitted some details including maternal cannibalism in a city under siege, but sufficiently frightening for the purpose. There are more biblical texts in this ritual than in any of the others; on the subjects of devastation and hope they are incomparable and inexhaustible.

The Jewish festival of Shavuot can fall no later than the week before the summer solstice, though like most Jewish holidays it has no conscious seasonal content. Nevertheless the notion of the law being given in fire and smoke *in summer* is arresting. To the American temperate-zone sensibility in which summer is the time of school vacation, relaxation, swimming and games, the conjunction may open a new way of thinking, or reawaken an old one. Summer vacation was originally established to accommodate agriculture; the law of survival took precedence even over the transmission of literacy.

To be held on the night of the summer solstice; in the far north, to be held at midnight. The dance at the end should be complex and well rehearsed (non-dancers can be spectators): less energetic than morris dancing given the hotter weather, but with the same sense that the season cannot be ushered in without the proper performance of the ritual.

Choose one of the Invocations, pp. 20–24.

Earth:

> Let the heavens rejoice and the earth be glad; let the sea and all within it thunder; let the fields exult, and all that is in them; let all the trees of the wood rejoice, because the earth will be judged.

Air:

> The power which causes the several portions of the plant to help each other we call life. Much more is this so in an animal. We may take away the branch of a tree without much harm to it; but not the animal's limb. Intensity of life is also intensity of helpfulness—completeness of depending of each part on all the rest. The ceasing of this help is what we call corruption; and in proportion to the perfectness of the help is the dreadfulness of the loss.

Water:

> What would the world be, once bereft
> Of wet and of wildness? Let them be left,
> O let them be left, wildness and wet;
> Long live the weeds and the wilderness yet.

Fire:

> The sun comes forth like a bridegroom out of his chamber; it rejoices like a strong man to run a race; nothing is hid from its heat.

Quintessence:

> The flintstone that is being rubbed in order to make it luminous understands what is being demanded of it, and its brilliance proves its condescension. How should the minerals do us so much good through their virtues without enjoying the sweet satisfaction,

the gentle satisfaction which is the first and greatest reward for beneficence?

All:

The highest and first law of the universe, and the other name of life, is "help."

Quintessence:

From whence comes our help? And can help fail?

All:

Let all the folk of the world beware, because the earth will be judged.

Quintessence:

What will become of us in that day?

All:

Woe to you who desire that day. Why do you seek that day? It is darkness and not light.

Quintessence:

    The day the misused ore absconds
(From every jukebox, laundromat, motel
One melting, sabotaging, homesick flow)
Back, back into mines virginal once more.

All (singing):

Where will our sadness hide
    In that day, in that day,
Where will our sadness hide
    In that day?
Our errors shall be tried

And justice shall be cried
And shall not be denied
   In that day, in that day,
And shall not be denied
   In that day.

Earth:

And the earth shall be judged: with plague, with fever, with burning heat, with thirst and with the sword, with blasting winds and with withering. And the locust shall eat all the trees and fruit of your land, until you are destroyed and perish quickly.

Water:

See, waters are rising from the North, and shall become an overflowing flood, and shall overwhelm the land and all that is in it, the city and all its inhabitants.

Air:

The skies over your head shall be brass, and the earth beneath you iron. The rain shall be powder and dust.

Fire:

You who live carelessly, who say in your heart, "I am, and none but me," who say, "No one can see me": evil shall come upon you which you cannot forestall. The day comes that shall burn like an oven; all the proud and all that do evil shall be stubble. The day that is coming shall burn them up and leave neither root nor branch.

Quintessence:

> And as the world strengthened and multiplied you, so it will starve and diminish you, and waste you from off the land. You shall be scattered and shall have no rest; you shall have a trembling heart and dazed eyes and sorrow of mind. In the morning you shall say, "Who will give back last night?" and in the evening you shall say, "Who will give back this morning?" for what your heart shall fear and your eyes shall see. You shall become an astonishment, and a proverb, and a byword. And you shall be left few in number, who were as many as the stars in the skies.

All turn to face outward from the circle.

All:

> Turn us again and we shall be turned; renew our days as of old.

Earth:

> Who speaks of the eternal return? Every return is temporary. Once for everything, only once; once and no more.

Water:

> And we too, once. Never again. But to have been this once, even if only once, to have been on the earth, this cannot be repealed.

All:

> Set the law of help in our inward parts, and write it on our hearts, to ransom all that stands in danger.

Air:

> Call on the wind, call it from the four corners, and let it breathe on the slain.

Fire:

> The parched ground shall become a pool, and the thirsty land springs of water; the abode of jackals shall be grassland with reeds and rushes. The wilderness and the wasteland shall be glad; the desert shall rejoice, and blossom like the rose.

All:

> And the remnant that escapes shall yet take root downward and bear fruit upward.

Quintessence:

> How shall these things be?

All turn back again to face each other across the circle.

All:

> Only through intelligence: through the intellect of love that moves in all matter, of which we are the inexpert keepers.

Quintessence:

> Listen, all you who wrestle with your fate: the intimate and the infinite are one.

All:

> Desire that union with your whole heart, doubt and all; with your whole soul, and with all your powers. Remember it: repeat it everywhere, working or

resting, sitting or walking, night and morning, alone and together. See it written on your hand, on your brow, in every common place and in every face.

Quintessence:

We think we will go unnoticed, that we will pass and leave no trace; but that which planted the ear, shall it not hear? and that which made the eye, shall it not see?

All:

That which jointed the thumbs and woke the mind, let it establish the work of our hands. Every atom is in full energy, and all that energy is kind.

A dance to a wordless round, so that the help of all the parts is needed to supply the whole.

The Conclusion (p. 25) is read.

Notes

*Let the heavens rejoice...*Ps. 96, 11-13.

The power which causes.... John Ruskin, "The Law of Help," in *Modern Painters* v. 5 (slightly altered).

What would the world be... Gerard Manley Hopkins, "*Inversnaid.*"

*The sun comes forth...*Ps. 19, 6-7.

The flintstone... J.-B. Robinet, *De la nature*, 1766, quoted in Gaston Bachelard, *The Psychoanalysis of Fire* (Boston: Beacon Press, 1964), 30.

The highest and first law...is "help." Ruskin, *op. cit.*

From whence comes our help? Ps. 121:1, adapted.

Woe to you... Amos 5:18.

the day the misused ore absconds... Peter Viereck, *The Tree Witch* (NY: Scribners, 1961), 70.

Where will our sadness hide... The Sacred Harp song "Wondrous Love" provides a suitable tune for this verse.

And the earth shall be judged... All lines not otherwise identified in this section are freely adapted from Deuteronomy 28.

See, waters are rising... Jer. 47:2.

You who live carelessly...cannot forestall. Isa. 47:8-14, adapted.

The day comes... Mal. 4:1, adapted.

Turn us again... Lam. 5:21.

Once for everything...cannot be repealed. Rainer Maria Rilke, "Ninth Duino Elegy," my (rough) translation.

Set the law of help... Jer. 31:33, adapted.

Call on the wind... Ezek. 37:9, adapted.

The parched ground...reeds and rushes. Isa. 35:7.

The wilderness and the wasteland... Isa. 35:1, adapted.

And the remnant... Isa. 37:31.

How shall these things be? Luke 1:34, adapted.

The intellect of love. Dante, *La Vita Nuova*, first *canzone*: *"Donne ch' avete intelletto d' amore..."*

Listen, all you...every face. An impressionistic translation of the *Shema Yisrael*, Deut. 6:4-9.

That which planted...shall it not see? Ps. 94:9.

Every atom is in full energy... Ruskin, *op. cit.*

Bible translations consulted: the King James Version; *Torah Neviim Ketuvim: The Holy Scriptures* (Jerusalem: Koren, 1977); *Tanakh: The Holy Scriptures* (Philadelphia: Jewish Publication Society, 1985); *Tyndale's Old Testament*, ed. David Daniell (New Haven: Yale University Press, 1992); *Tanach: The Stone Edition*, ed. Nosson Scherman (Brooklyn: Mesorah, 1996).

Harvest

In old Celtic paganism, the festival of Lammas was the midpoint between the summer solstice and the fall equinox. In 1945 at this time of year, nature and history intersected with particular force in the bombing of Hiroshima and Nagasaki. The timing of any act of war is coincident with the seasons only as the seasons may interfere with or permit it; yet almost immediately our sense of pattern takes over, and we insist on seeing meaning or paradox. The Jewish fast day of Tisha b'Av, which mourns the destruction of the Temple in Jerusalem, also falls at about this point.

Perhaps this ritual was outdated even as it was written; nuclear proliferation is dwarfed by the magnitude of ecological breakdown. In retrospect it seems far easier for political leaders to refrain from "pushing the button" than for the human race in general to reformulate all our uses of fuel in response to a hypothesis that we all hope is not true. Still, there is one thing common to both crises: the undercurrent of knowledge among civilians that their civilian status will not spare them. For all the hype and nonsense that is talked about the "baby boom" generation, a mass of people who grew up in the wake of mass killing know that any mass of people, including themselves, is dispensable.

To be held on August 6. The ritual begins with a procession: the Elements and the people bearing various produce of the season, oil and vinegar and herbs, and bread and wine.

All (singing):

> All I love, all I have,
> Green one, from the grave you give.

Choose one of the Invocations, pp. 20–24.

Quintessence:

> This is the feast of the first fruits, the mutual triumph
> of the gardener and the plant. All people everywhere
> who have farmed have kept the harvest, and bread
> and wine have always been holy foods. They have sig-
> naled the mystery of fruition and fermentation; they
> have signified the transmutation of food into God;
> they have been occasion for blessing and gratitude.
> But today we eat and drink them out of triumph:
> that we and the wheat and the vine so managed it, so
> changed the harshness of the elements into kindness,
> that we all lived. Blessed be all that effort that stood
> against death.

All:

> What they undertook to do
> They brought to pass;
> All things hang like a drop of dew
> Upon a blade of grass.

The Elements take the bread and wine to pass, but the Quintessence prevents them.

Quintessence:

> Not yet. There is another harvest we remember at
> this time. A dark harvest, mirroring the bright one
> as blindness mirrors sight. Not a turning in the year,
> but a turning in history.

*The **Elements** put the food down and cover their eyes.*

Earth:

> At that time earth was not the matrix of life but the congealment of terror.

Water:

> Water was the liquefaction of fear.

Air:

> Air was the flight of grief.

Fire:

> Fire was the raging of death, annihilating all.

Quintessence:

> The human intelligence had discovered a new death, and the years since have multiplied its dangers.

Fire:

> We had learned in Europe, and we learned again in Japan, that nothing is forbidden: not because everything is permitted, but because nothing is prevented.

*The **Elements** uncover their eyes.*

All:

> How doth the city sit solitary, that was full of people! How is she become as a widow! She that was great among the nations, and princess among the provinces, how is she become tributary! She weepeth sore in

the night, and her tears are on her cheeks; among all her lovers she hath none to comfort her.

Air:

The minds of great thinkers and healers were put to the service of generals; and then the minds of all three were put to the service of politicians; and at last all science and medicine and strategy became subject to the arrogance of windy fools.

Water:

And the degradation continues. Our leaders have spent our taxes making weapons that must not be used, while the poor go hungry and ignorant in the streets.

All:

What they undertook to do they brought to pass.

Earth:

And the great destruction threatens always: from constituted nations and from conspiracies, by plan or by accident, with warning or without warning.

Quintessence:

As the farmer must renew the soil for the sake of later harvests, so we must renew the mind against this great erosion; for it must someday produce a deliverance, a recovery, of the same magnitude as the worst of our destructions.

All:

All things hang like a drop of dew upon a blade of grass.

Quintessence:

> Now bless the wine and the bread, knowing their meaning: that we have escaped the destruction another year; that the world still bears, and we are its burden.

The Elements pass the bread and wine around the circle.

Earth:

> Eat the bread, simple and savored;

Water:

> Drink the wine, subtle and strong;

Air:

> Earliest and kindest of transformations:

Fire:

> The staff of life and the soother of pain.

Quintessence:

> Transform their substance into your own, with a merciful intelligence and the wisdom of restraint, that each of us who has power to destroy withhold destruction; that we offer to all what we receive today: the simple magnificence of continuing to live.

All take the produce and make it into a salad, of which everyone takes a share.

The Conclusion (p. 25) is read.

Notes

All I love... Vernon Watkins, "Secrecy," in *The Ballad of the Outer Dark* (London: Enitharmon Press, 1979), 17.

What they undertook... W. B. Yeats, "Gratitude to the Unknown Instructors."

At that time...annihilating all. Adapted from Irenaeus of Lyon, *Adversus Haereses* I.5.4, qtd. in Hans Jonas, *The Gnostic Religion* (Boston: Beacon Press, 1963), 189.

How doth the city... Lamentations 1:1-2.

Fall Equinox

The most obvious influence on this ritual is Yom Kippur: the confession of damage done, the fiction of an annual reckoning and a symbolic confrontation with death, and the prostration before a presence that cannot be named but that offers (at least emblematically) a way out of our errors. Having served many times since writing this ritual as cantor at Yom Kippur services, I notice the stylistic differences as clearly as the influences; in its shortness and coherence this ritual has a certain intensity, but the sheer cumbrous weight of the day-long fast and the many reiterations of the established Jewish liturgy are a more taxing ordeal. Yom Kippur also, in a sense, intends itself as an ordeal for God: a battery of confessions and prayers that will compel his forgiveness. If, in the religion of nature, forgiveness is not imaginable, there remains the hope that repentance (or "turning"), along with prayer and acts of mercy, may temper the severity of cause and effect.

To be held at twilight on the evening of the fall equinox.

Choose one of the Invocations, pp. 20–24.

Quintessence:

> On this day, day and night stand equal in the sky. Time crosses its own path, as the fall equinox repeats the spring. The universe hints at equity, and at amendment: that the rashness of growth is atoned for in the time of waning, and the harm done in the green tree may be repaired in the dry.

Earth:

> We have troubled the earth, by abusing the soil and scattering poisons; and we have troubled the body, despising its humble tenderness and exhausting it for purposes we do not love.

All:

> We have stopped short of kindness, and the world's heart is broken.

Water:

> We have tainted the water, by sending all wastes into it without distinction; and we have tainted feeling by fouling it with indulgence, the petty beside the noble without distinction.

All:

> We have stopped short of honor, and the world's heart is broken.

Air:

> We have damaged the air, by the vapors of our chemistry and the smoke of our burnings; and we have damaged the intellect, by not holding it crucial as breath.

All:

> We have stopped short of intelligence, and the world's heart is broken.

Fire:

> We have wasted fire, using it for every need without imagination or limit; and we have wasted the soul, dulling it by habit and incuriosity.

All:

> We have stopped short of awe, and the world's heart is broken.

Quintessence:

> We have hindered the work of creation. We grieve for the hurts we have given others; we suffer the hurts we have taken; we crave that through all this giving of pain there may be some justice and some mercy that returns us to each other kindly.

*The following litany is read in call-and-response, alternating lines being read by the **Elements** and the people.*

> From the harm we have done through power and the harm we have done through powerlessness, turn us again.

> *From the harm we have done knowingly and the harm we have done unknowingly, turn us again.*

> From the harm we have done for truth's sake and the harm we have done without truth, turn us again.

> *From the harm we have done from cowardice and the harm we have done from courage, turn us again.*

From the harm we have done from hatred and the harm we have done from love, turn us again.

From the harm we have done for beauty's sake and the harm we have done against beauty, turn us again.

From the harm we have done from eagerness and the harm we have done from reluctance, turn us again.

From the harm we have done through heaviness of spirit and the harm we have done through lightness of mind, turn us again.

From the harm we have done and been found out, and the harm that remains secret, turn us again.

From the harm we have done for a reason, and the harm we have done for no reason, turn us again.

Quintessence:

These are the ways we earn death. Death comes to us in the course of nature, but these are the ways we deserve it.

All:

Why, in the course of nature, does ignorance weigh heavy as knowledge?

Why do our acts return to us, even those done without knowledge?

Why, as we labor against misery in one place, do we create it again in another?

Why are our wrongs irretrievable, and their effects never ended?

Why are our deeds indelible, not only the good but the evil, standing forever against us in the book of the past?

Why was the world born broken, and all our efforts to mend it made subject to decay?

Quintessence:

Why were we given such hopelessness, that in one long history still unfolding, in one train of actions linked together, we should have one chance to act and act wrongly?

All:

Why do we who are dust have such power?

Quintessence:

In the darkness, before anything was, nothing longed to become something; and from that longing came matter out of spirit, life from the inert, history from the unremembered, and the finite from the infinite. All that is imaginable began to be imagined. Who can tell if that longing was fulfilled?—whether the world that appeared was the world that was longed for? Who can tell if that longing sprang from exuberance or pain?

All:

But this we understand: we are not free of that longing. We want to bring the world into being. Give us, Nameless, out of the midst, the word of beginning: the word that heals shame, that pardons error, that gives strength against terror, that restores the soul; that teaches wisdom, that enlightens the dark, that lives forever, that rejoices the heart.

*All prostrate themselves. After a time of silence, a **Singer** rises and begins to sing, the **Elements** and the people gradually rising and humming a background of harmonies to the song.*

Singer:

> I know moonlight,
> I know starlight,
> I lay this body down.
>
> I walk in the moonlight,
> I walk in the starlight,
> I lay this body down.
>
> I know the morning
> And the evening star,
> I lay this body down.
>
> Oh, graveyard,
> Oh, graveyard,
> I lay this body down.
>
> I walk in the graveyard,
> I lay in my grave,
> I lay this body down.
>
> I lay in my grave,
> I feel my grave's side,
> I lay this body down.
>
> I go to the judgment
> In the evening of the day
> When I lay this body down.
>
> Then my soul and your soul
> Will meet on that day
> When I lay this body down.
>
> I know moonlight,
> I know starlight,
> I lay this body down.

Quintessence:

> Speak us like a language, O breath of life: whisper us
> into the void, and we shall be spoken. Let our shame
> not silence you, as though a singer should hate the
> sound of her own voice and recant of singing; give us
> utterance, and we shall be heard.

Stepping into the center of the circle and extending one hand:

> Come, dear friends, partners in uncertainty:
> Come and tread the measure of infinity.
> Time waits for you: come and establish equity.

The **Quintessence** *leads the people through the center of the circle and
into a figure eight or infinity symbol (∞), through which they move for
several turns as the following song is sung. At the crossing point of the
figure eight, the people drop hands and cross one by one, so that each
moves alone through the space between two others in the opposite line.*

Elements (singing):

> When to the new eyes of thee
> all things by immortal power
> > near and far,
> > hiddenly,
> to each other linkèd are
> that thou canst not stir a flower
> without troubling of a star,
> > from that hour,
> > haltingly,
> learn the language of repair.

The Conclusion (p. 25) is read.

Notes

The harm done in the green tree may be repaired in the dry. A play on
  Luke 23:31.

From the harm we have done... Influenced by the *Al ḥet* in the Yom
  Kippur liturgy.

In the darkness... Influenced by Jakob Böhme and the Zohar.

The word that heals shame... After Ps. 19:7-9.

I know moonlight... African-American spiritual. This version from
  the singing of Helen Bonchek Schneyer, *On the Hallelujah
  Line* (Folk-Legacy FSI–85).

When to the new eyes... Francis Thompson, "The Mistress of
  Vision." The last three lines are my own revision.

Allhallows

Readers of Harold Bloom will appreciate why I first thought of calling this ritual "The Feast of the Transumption." I borrowed from him the notion that we absorb the work of the dead into our own work, yet also bend it to our own purposes. We know well enough that even altruism can have a strong degree of ego in it; as self-consciously moral beings we like the look of ourselves as moral, as rescuers and defenders. Nevertheless there are occasions when people need rescue and defense, whether we congratulate ourselves on it or not.

Nothing in the seasonal rituals seemed to me less promising than to try to make Halloween a day seriously devoted to the subject of rescue, and to the dead of the twentieth century. Ghosts and goblins and trick-or-treating, the merry guitar-playing skeletons of the *Día de los Muertos*, mentioned in the same breath with the slaughtered soldiers of the First World War, the victims of Hitler and Stalin and Pol Pot? All Saints' Day has the requisite gravity, but confines itself to the saints; the characterizing horror of twentieth-century mass death was its indiscrimination. In the end I borrowed from the Jewish tradition at Sukkot of inviting the *ushpizin*, the ancestors, into the family sukkah. People estranged from religion may need, to some extent, to adopt their ancestors: to consider who their dead are, and how to become worthy of them. (My essay "The Unquiet Grave" approaches this subject and may interest some readers; it is now posted at

http://www.earthspirit.com/fireheart/fhuqg.)

Earth, air, fire and water are, I read somewhere, the four means of disposing of the dead: burial, exposure, cremation and sea-burial.

*To be held on the night of October 31. As the people enter the circle, the person reading the part of **Earth** marks their foreheads with a thumb-smear of oil—patchouli, vetivert or some other earthy scent.*

*Choose one of the Invocations, pp. 20-24; or the ritual may begin without preface, using the **Elements'** first statements as invocations.*

Earth:

The earth is full of graves.

Air:

The air heavy with ashes.

Fire:

The fire has eaten our lovers.

Water:

The water swallowed them up.

Quintessence:

By the endless designs of the fifth, that devises death for the people: that devises a death for each one that enters the world alive.

All:

Daily we eat and drink and breathe our dead; nightly we are gathered to our dead in sleep. But tonight we speak to them. Tonight the nation of the living greets the nation of the dead.

Quintessence:

> When we were young, people frightened us on this night, kindly and within limits. But we knew then, and we know now, that there are fears without limit. It is not the ghosts of the dead we fear, but the acts of the living. Not the skeleton, but the allegiance that demands the skeleton; not decay, but the agony that precedes decay; not the dead, but the living who have no pity.

All:

> We who have survived to this time must do what the dead cannot: we must work to dispel fear.

All are seated. Wine is poured for everyone in the circle, and an extra cup for the ancestors is placed in the center.

Quintessence:

> We drink to the lives of the lost.

All:

> May they persist in us.

All drink the wine.

Earth:

> A time will come when we will beat our senses into recollections, and all time into the past. A time will come when a single past will embrace us all, when there will be nothing except the past, when everyone will have one faith—the past.

Water:

> In each age, the number of the dead, that dark society, acts on the living with the force of an increasing majority working out its affirmations, asserting its preferences ever more and more distinctly, and with more completely universal assent.

Air:

> A skull is more lasting than any theology; and one man's bones will outlive a dozen systems of philosophy.

Fire:

> If we, as we are, are dust, and dust, as it will, rises,
> Then we will rise, and recongregate
> In the wind, in the cloud, and be their issue.

*All begin to hum together softly. Gradually the sound builds in volume and diversifies into a complex discord; if the **Elements** begin this process, people unfamiliar with it will learn it easily. At the height of the sound, **Earth**, **Air**, **Fire** and **Water** burst out of the circle and fling open the doors and windows, singing):*

Elements:

> Beloved, holy dead, come to us!
> From dust and ashes come to us!
> From wind and water come to us!
> Witnesses and judges, come to us!

Quintessence (raising the extra cup of wine):

> Come to us, teach us, remember us!

*The other **Elements** close the doors and windows and return to their places masked, sitting among the others. The **Quintessence** takes the ancestors' cup to each of them in silence.*

Quintessence:

> O our beloved dead, who are present but silent, what would you say to us if you could speak?

All:

> We live in a dark age, as none know better than your-selves, and the future is full of doubt.

Quintessence:

> We fear that we will find no remedy for the world's pain: that neither the effort to heal each other's suf-fering nor the effort to escape our own is of any use.

All:

> The year gathers darkness, and we are full of fear; where shall we find hope?

Earth:

> Distinguish. The year gathers darkness, but every year gathers darkness: darkness is not an evil.

Water:

> Distinguish between natural darkness and hell. There is the eclipse of light that comes from the turning of the earth toward winter; winter is not an evil. But there is also the annihilation of light that comes from ignorance, and that is a great evil.

Air:

> Material darkness turns again towards light; intellectual darkness spreads itself further, eradicating hope.

Fire:

> The darkness of the tormentor is less than the darkness of the tormented. The tormentor is ignorant of the weight of harsh deeds; the tormented bears that knowledge, and is crushed by the burden.

Quintessence:

> In the confrontation of the gentle with the brutal, the gentle will always lose; always unless someone turn and protect it. We have not discovered the way to prevent the cruel from cruelty.

Elements:

> But cruelty may be averted, one act at a time.

Quintessence:

> Let us name those in whose memory we will protect.

Each person in the circle names someone among the dead in whose name and memory he or she will work for the coming year.

All (*one by one*):

> Remember *N.*, and I will remember *him/her;* for *his/ her* sake I will not turn from pain.

All (*each time, answering*):

> We will remember.

When All have spoken, the Elements continue:

Elements:

> You will not remember. You will take our work and turn it to some other purpose; you will take our names and make them echoes of your own.

All:

> No: your fate has moved us, and we want to do your work. Graft your lives on the cloven stock of our souls, and we will grow your way and not our own.

Elements:

> But the soul is wild and returns to its own growth in a new year. You will do your own work, even when you think it ours. You will do our work only when you do not know it. (*Standing*) You are not required to complete the work, but neither are you free to desist from it. And if you too are defeated by others' inhumanity, think that defeat no refutation.

All (*standing*):

> Will shall be the sterner, heart the bolder,
> Spirit the greater as our strength lessens.
> Mind shall not falter nor mood waver,
> Though doom shall come and dark conquer.

Elements:

> So be it.

The Elements leave the circle, open the doors and windows, and remove their masks.

All:

> You who now rest in earth, in air, in fire, in water:
> teach us to go to the end of our destiny, neither to
> recoil from it nor to perish untimely. Haunt us with
> the longing for justice.

*The **Elements** return unmasked to the circle, and the Conclusion (p. 25) is read.*

Notes

Daily we eat...in sleep. John Cowper Powys, *The Art of Happiness* (New York: Simon and Schuster, 1935), 93.

A time will come... Elias Canetti, *Auto-da-Fé* (New York: Farrar Straus Giroux, 1984), 159 (slightly adapted).

In each age... Walter Pater, qtd. in Harold Bloom, *The Breaking of the Vessels* (Chicago: University of Chicago Press, 1982), 39.

A skull is more lasting... John Cowper Powys, *A Philosophy of Solitude* (New York: Simon and Schuster, 1933), 211.

If we, as we are, are dust... Charles Wright, "Snow," in *China Trace* (Middletown, CT: Wesleyan University Press. 1977), 14.

Beloved, holy dead... Influenced by the *Ushpizin* in the Sukkot service.

Remember N... Influenced by the Yizkor service.

You are not required...to desist from it. Pirke Avot 2:21.

And if you too are defeated... Influenced by W. P. Ker's description of the gods of Norse mythology, who "are on the right side, though it is not the side that wins. The winning side is Chaos and Unreason, but the gods, who are defeated, think that defeat no refutation." Qtd. in J. R. R. Tolkien, "The Monsters and the Critics," in *An Anthology of Beowulf Criticism*, ed. Lewis E. Nicholson (Notre Dame, Indiana: Notre Dame University Press, 1963), 70.

Will shall be the sterner... J. R. R. Tolkien, "The Homecoming of Beorhtnoth Beorhthelm's Son," in *The Tolkien Reader* (New York: Ballantine, 1966). The first two lines are taken from the introductory essay (5) and the last two from the play itself (17).

to go to the end of our destiny...perish untimely. Olivier Revault d'Allonnes, *Musical Variations on Jewish Thought*, trans. Judith L. Greenberg (New York: George Braziller, 1984), 80-81.

Possible models for the maskmaker to follow are Käthe Kollwitz, Leonard Baskin, Georges Jeanclos; the faces should suggest strangeness and tragedy but also intimacy, likeness to ourselves.

Prayers

Prayers for Various Occasions

Of the making of many prayers there is no end; this is a random assortment. It seems impossible to avoid entirely the language of request, even while not insisting that someone is there to answer. Though petitionary prayer, when taken literally as a *quid pro quo*, seems servile and ineffective, the real point of the phenomenon is probably not its efficacy. Rather it is a convulsive necessity, in which one does not ask a benign and trusted God for something that will surely be given, but begs the future to yield an outcome one dare not be sure of. We can hold in our minds with no trouble both the rational impossibility of imagining a good (or even an evil) God in charge of all this, and the simultaneous necessity to say "thank you" or "damn you" or "can't you?" to *something* at critical moments. We send our words out into nowhere; sometimes nowhere appears to listen, and sometimes not.

On waking:

O great radiance, daily renewed, burn me without consuming.

On seeing sunrise or sunset:

How earth and water adore the sky, and how the sky desires them; how the earth lies open to the heavens, and still water longs to mirror light.

Twice a day, implacably, dawn and dusk are given. We creatures of flesh and leaf, that make ourselves out of the inanimate, transform continually the implacable into the tender. But the inanimate shows us the way. The implacable is also the tender. Blessed at morning and evening be the mercy of pale light.

On seeing the moon:

Old stone that floats over the night lands, we re-member.

During a snowstorm:

Blessed among all weather is the snowfall, that by crowding the air reveals it, and by covering the earth discloses it: definer of surfaces, angel of edges, bring-er of peace.

On seeing a place damaged by erosion or pollution:

Where I have always looked for peace, there is no peace: the signs of unraveling are everywhere. Old sorrow, old moan of roots in the ground, how we in-crease you.

On looking at a beloved person:

May the planes of this face and the texture of this skin be indelible in air forever.

Against shame:

My own heart let me more have pity on; let
Me live to my sad self hereafter kind,
Charitable; not live this tormented mind
With this tormented mind tormenting yet.
— Gerard Manley Hopkins

For endurance in physical or mental pain:

> The Chemical conviction
> That Nought be lost
> Enable in Disaster
> My fractured Trust—
>
> — Emily Dickinson

On taking medicine or undergoing medical treatment whose outcome is unknown:

> Behold, thou desirest truth in the inward parts; and in the hidden part thou shalt make me to know wisdom.
>
> — Psalm 51:6

Survivor's prayer:

> I am re-begot
> Of absence, darkness, death: things which are not.
> Surely my help is here, and I knew it not.
>
> (The first two lines are from John Donne, "A nocturnall upon *S. Lucies* day, Being the shortest day"; the third is adapted from Genesis 28:16.)

Against religious hatred:

> Let me not despise anyone because of religion. We are all mortals together. This is the faith that underlies all religion: the truth of the body, the passing of time, and the will of the people toward one another.

Against racial and ethnic hatred:

> Turn us from the long curse of our kind, the war between peoples. While we run after our hatreds, the world melts.

Against despair in family life or workplace:

> I am bound without remedy to people I do not trust.
> This bond may cripple me, but it will not corrupt me;
> I will not forfeit judgment for the relief of despising
> them.
>
> The people who oppress me are also souls, full of
> private tenderness and bitterness as I am. Let me not
> turn from them in contempt and rage, but remember
> their weakness. Let the simplicity of what we hold in
> common return us to each other.

Gratitude for one's family or beloved people:

> What mercy has given me to you? Let me be worthy
> to live next to your lives.

Prayers for Women

Other subjects than women's biological occasions, and other views of these subjects, are of course possible; I am taking no position on the scope of "women's issues," merely writing what seemed interesting to me under the pressure of a great deal of feminist liturgy.

Charm for pregnancy:

Come, quicken, sicken me, thrive,
Dream in my blood; be born alive.

Mourning charm, for miscarriage:

Little knot, little knot, soon severed
seed on the dull earth scattered
go where my dead are gathered
measure of sorrow measured

A vow not to have children:

Let the generations of my body cease with me: let them not be born so that others may have room. What I give to the future is my lifetime's work and the empty space ahead of me. Let my barrenness restore some other's garden.

Prayers for abortion:

Before the abortion, the woman goes alone to a dark room, lights one candle, and placing her hands on her belly, says:

In the bitter choices of this world, let me not fail from responsibility, let me not fail from compassion. Let me cede this choice to no other.

Child, let us understand each other: you wish for life, but I must not give it to you. If this world were a wider place I would make your way gentle; but my way is hard and narrow, and I walk it alone. This is my choice where there are no good choices, that the world be less full of desperation.

She pinches out the flame between finger and thumb.

When she has recovered from the abortion she says, holding her empty hands before her:

Nothing is lost, not even the broken, not even the ruined, not even the shamed. I who might have been this child's mother and am not, am changed: the death of a small thing is on me and must be made good. Let me turn from abdication and aimlessness, doing what I greatly desire and honor, no lesser substitute.

(*Nothing is lost...not even the ruined* is borrowed, with a change of syntax and context, from Alice Bloch's *The Law of Return* [Boston: Alyson, 1983], 229.)

Rites of Passage

Individual rites of passage present a different set of problems for the writer than seasonal rituals—particularly in disorganized religion, where the nature of groups is to form and dissolve rapidly. Seasonal rituals (and private prayers) are designed for repetition over a period of years; a particular rite of passage occurs once in a person's life. A cohesive and long-enduring community might see several cycles of baby-naming, coming of age, marriage, divorce, illness and death, but there will always be friends and relatives present who are not part of the group; somehow the rituals must be made intelligible to them as well. Thus these rites of passage approach more directly than the seasonal rituals one of the fundamental questions of liturgy: What kind of people are we trying to make? Where the seasonal rituals speak of communal and planetary dilemmas, the rites of passage speak of individual and private ones.

The examples that follow are more or less conventional in their outlines. The marriage service, for example, is for two partners, though I have not specified their genders. Unconventional situations of various kinds do mark themselves with ritual, but such rituals have a specificity and a privacy beyond the scope of this book; the more uncommon the circumstances, the more important (and the more possible) it is to write them into the ritual in the imaginative idiom of the person or persons involved. That is to say, rituals for unusual circumstances must be tailored to the people who need them, and thus cannot be offered for general use. They may also need to remain unpublished during the lifetimes of those concerned. The general methods used here—concentration, intensity, allusiveness—serve in those circumstances as well, and for the same purpose: to contain and support strong emotion.

Naming a Baby

It may take a certain emotional endurance to use this ritual, but it takes a good deal more to raise a child; it may be useful, at the outset and in ritual form, to consider the outline of a life as it develops, and the nature of a parent's charge. Euphoria and humility, confidence and foreboding, all come with the job. The ritual is written as if for a family with both parents present, but may be fairly easily adapted to other configurations. Social patterns of childrearing may change; what does not change is physical and cognitive development, the need to accommodate the child while teaching the child how to accommodate others.

I have made no provision, and perhaps I should, for the hazards of parental ill-treatment: for extreme or violent punishment, habitual verbal abuse, incest, neglect. It is hard to imagine what words might reach beneath the level of these instinctual misfires, which themselves proceed from great pain and a fathomless sense of incapacity. What memorable preliminary ordeal could possibly offset the present reality of the sleepless infant or the intractable child, poverty or the fear of it, the disorienting effects of drink or drugs, the effects of violence done to the parent in childhood, or the simple fury at being the helpless guardian of a helpless being? Perhaps an oath: *If I strike him, may I be stricken.*

*The parents bring the baby outside in procession with friends and relations, five of whom will represent the **Elements**. Someone goes before them sprinkling a pathway of seeds (grass seed or flowers or anything* *that will sprout up and leave evidence of their having been there). They form a circle and the parents hold the baby up in the center.*

Parents:

> Friends and relations, sun and wind, and all things that stand within our sight: see, here is our *son/daughter N.*, who was not and now is, and we made *him/her!* Bless *his/her* coming into the world, and help us to raise *him/her* well.

All:

> We will strengthen you. Bless your will to begin and your courage to continue.

Parents:

> Elements of life, bless our child with your dangerous wisdom.

The Elements come forward out of the circle one by one to touch the baby and bless it.

Earth:

> Each mortal thing does one thing and the same:
> Deals out that being indoors each one dwells;
> Selves—goes itself: *myself* it speaks and spells;
> Crying *What I do is me: for that I came.*

Water:

> Surely whoever speaks to me in the right voice, him
>   or her shall I follow,
> As the water follows the moon, silently, with fluid
>   steps anywhere around the globe.

Air:

> Seek those images
> That constitute the wild,
> The lion and the virgin,
> The harlot and the child.
>
> Find in middle air
> An eagle on the wing,
> Recognize the five
> That make the Muses sing.

Fire:

> Lest we should see too much and burn
> Our human natures clean away
> By feeling more than we can bear,
> We blindfold every night and day,
> Of all but fragments unaware.
>
> This is the School of Babylon
> And at its hands we learn
> To walk into the furnaces
> And whistle as we burn.

Quintessence:

> The angel that presided o'er my birth
> Said, Little creature, formed of joy and mirth,
> Go love without the help of any thing on earth.

Parents:

> These are the conditions by which our child lives. We
> cannot refuse them, but we can enlarge them:
>
> for where you give exuberance, we will give shape;
> where you give revelation, we will give steadiness;
> where you give wings, we will give anchors;

where you give terror, we will give courage;
where you give loneliness, we will give home.

Speaking to the baby:

Little soul, new to the world, little place where there
was no place: may we be strong enough for your
strength, and worthy of your trust, and may we make
no error too great for your pardon. Welcome to the
world!

Notes

The idea of the pathway of seeds was suggested by an adaptation
of a Hopi ritual by Sheila Ritter and Mark Charles.

Each mortal thing... Gerard Manley Hopkins, "As Kingfishers
Catch Fire."

Surely whoever speaks... Walt Whitman, "Vocalism," in *Leaves of
Grass.*

Seek those images... W. B. Yeats, "Those Images."

Lest we should see... Thomas Blackburn, "The School of Babylon,"
in *Selected Poems* (London: Hutchinson, 1975), 40.

The angel that presided... William Blake, fragment from the MS.
notebook of 1808–11, in *Complete Writings,* ed. Geoffrey
Keynes (Oxford: Oxford University Press, 1972), 541.

Coming of Age

Few children who have actually prepared for bar or bat mitzvah will credit that I envy them. Nevertheless it is one of the main things I think Judaism gets right. An *intellectual* rite of passage at puberty—a rite that develops one's skill and speed with a radically different language and alphabet and system of musical notation, a rite that gives one the same public task as the most highly skilled adults in the congregation—every child needs such an opportunity, and its absence accounts for much alienation, abdication and violence among adolescents. What is the secular equivalent? Getting one's driver's license? Mastering the intricacies of personal grooming and the argot and dress code of one's peers? Children who are musicians or athletes are some of the luckiest, because they already have a demanding calling with set standards; children who tutor younger children are lucky too, in having a task that awakens their empathy and requires their imagination. Children who are socially isolated and uncertain of their work can easily despair of ever being heard or taken seriously. Withdrawal into some byway of popular culture only prolongs the sense of having no adult role, though it will seem a safe compromise for some. For others, dangerous risks—pregnancy, drugs, anorexia, gang membership, self-mutilation, crime—may seem the only recourse.

The self-consciously anthropological rites of menarche among modern feminists are possibly a step in the right direction, though I wonder if they really reduce a young girl's embarrassment about her body (*Aww, maa, do you have to tell all your friends?*).

But puberty is involuntary; what really needs to be engaged in pre-adolescence is the mind and the will. In traditional Judaism, the father of the bar mitzvah speaks a formula declaring himself no longer responsible for the boy's sins. What education, what cognitive breakthroughs do you need in order to be responsible for your own sins? How do you know what constitutes a sin, or know yourself capable of refusing it? Or—for those contrarians whose first impulse on being made responsible for their own sins is to go out and commit some—how do you sin selectively, and make your errors (as Joyce said) volitional, and the portals of discovery?

My attempt is clumsy, and in retrospect preaches too much; bar mitzvah accomplishes all this without ever saying so, through the process of setting the child a complex task in a social and tutorial network, using an uncensored biblical text.

This ritual may take place at puberty or at the arbitrary age of thirteen. In preparation for it, the child should choose an apprenticeship: a serious art, trade or job in which he or she will be taught and judged according to adult standards (technique, theory, the work's place in the community and its effects on the surrounding environment). The child should be introduced to others working in the same field, including authorities whenever possible, and encouraged to consult them (and anyone else who might be helpful or who might stand in the way). The apprenticeship need not lead directly into the person's life work, if he or she chooses differently later; the point is to begin as soon as possible doing work that is one's own and not simply homework or housework.

*The people gather in a circle. The **Initiate** and his or her parents wait in another room.*

All (*calling the* **Initiate**'*s name*):

> *N.,* come in! *N.,* come in! *N.,* come in! Take your
> place in creation.

The **Initiate** *walks in, between his/her parents. As they enter the circle, the* **Elements** *step forward and make a smaller circle in the center around the* **Initiate** *leaving the parents in the outer circle. The* **Elements** *should stand in the order of their speaking, so that during the investiture the* **Initiate** *will make a quarter-turn clockwise to face each one. For a girl, the first line of the following poem should, obviously, be amended to "woman.")*

Initiate:

> I am a man now.
> Pass your hand over my brow.
> You can feel the place where the brains grow.
>
> I am like a tree.
> From my top boughs I can see
> The footprints that led up to me.
>
> There is blood in my veins
> That has run clear of the stain
> Contracted in so many loins.
>
> Why, then, are my hands red
> With the blood of so many dead?
> Is this where I was misled?
>
> Why are my hands this way
> That they will not do as I say?
> Does no God hear when I pray?
>
> I have nowhere to go.
> The swift satellites show
> The clock of my whole being is slow.

It is too late to start
For destinations not of the heart.
I must stay here with my hurt.

Earth:

You enter today upon the state of *manhood/woman-
hood*. That is a state both of responsibility and helplessness: helplessness to repeal the conditions we are
given, and responsibility to mend them.

Water:

We are born human, but we must learn to be humane.

Air:

Parent and child cannot speak the truth to each other: they want to speak truth, but they are bound in a
terrible intimacy beyond the reach of truth. But now
that you are of age, discern the truth: trust your own
sorrow, mourn what you lack, and find beyond lack
the luck of your own work.

Fire:

Whether your hurt is healed or endures to the grave;
whether your bliss is accomplished or still eludes you:
these things lie partly within your will and partly
with chance. But we ask you now something that lies
wholly within your will. What have you chosen for
the first stage of your work?

*The **Initiate** explains the apprenticeship he or she has chosen, and shows
a piece of work already accomplished. All sing a wordless tune of con-
gratulation, instead of applause.*

Quintessence:

> Your effort is good. Now we invest you with your obligations.

*During the investiture, the **Initiate** turns to the **Element** that is speaking, and each **Element** kisses the **Initiate**'s lips after speaking.*

Earth:

> *There is no body distinct from the soul.*
> Your body's work and rest depend upon your decisions. Through your body you also comprehend the strength or frailty of others' bodies: who to fear and who to care for. And now that you are of age, you face the heaviest of all decisions: you can *beget/bear* children, and you must not do so until you have the patience to care for them and the means to keep them from want. Every act of the body is a word of the soul, and if the soul speaks rashly the body lives in misery.

Water:

> *Where there are no people, you be a person.*
> All of us are your fellow-mortals, deserving both the judgment and the pity that you yourself deserve. The words between us must be trustworthy. Do not speak out of hatred, and do not turn hatred on yourself. Never assume that another person knows and rejects your needs, and hurts you out of hatred; they may do so out of ignorance, for none knows what another feels without being told. And never believe that you are powerless against difficulty. If your family hurts you, or your school bores you, or your friends disappoint you, you need not simply suffer it: study the remedy, and ask for what you need until you receive it.

Air:

> *The more piety, the more skepticism.*
> People will offer you answers to your pain, a doctrine or a drug; some are sweet and soon over, others are strong and cling with a cruel grip. But while you follow your work, you will not credit these false comforts; let them pass, and keep faith with the true ones. Would you rather believe the unbelievable, or do the impossible?

Fire:

> *You are not required to complete the work, but neither are you free to desist from it.*
> Do the impossible; imagine beyond what is given, and give it your gifts; bring into being what was not.

Quintessence:

> *Be not afraid of the universe.*
> Life wants to live itself through you. Do not hide from its light. Do not smother that spark with indifference and despair. Your life is valid and beloved; the universe desires you to be.

At this point there is general cheering and celebration; then friends and relations who wish to make speeches or present gifts do so. Then the Initiate says:

Initiate:

> Now I carry my life in my own hands. Help me, all of you, not to let it fall.

All:

With our own strength we will bear you up.

*The **Initiate**'s friends come forward, pick him/her up, and carry him/
her out of the circle.*

Notes

I am a man now... R. S. Thomas, "Here," in *Poems of R. S. Thomas*
(Fayetteville: University of Arkansas, 1985), 41-42.

There is no body distinct from the soul. William Blake, *The Marriage
of Heaven and Hell.*

Where there are no people, you be a person. Pirke Avot 2:6.

The more piety, the more skepticism. Cynthia Ozick, "The Pagan
Rabbi," in *The Pagan Rabbi and Other Stories* (New York:
Dutton, 1983), 25.

You are not required...to desist from it. Pirke Avot 2:21.

Be not afraid of the universe. The shaman Najagneq, qtd. in Joseph
Campbell, *The Masks of God: Primitive Mythology* (New York:
Viking, 1959), 350.

Questions for Couples Contemplating Marriage

There is something to be said for the view that marriage takes place in private, without benefit of clergy—that it is cemented by the couple at the point of mutual consent, or of consummation. The dress, the procession, the public vows, the party, all those celebratory markers of entrance on the married state, can too easily eclipse the state of mind in which we take another human being as husband or wife beyond celebration. The point at which any two people—with or without religious or legal sanction—become intimately committed to each other's bodies and futures may come before or well after the ritual of attachment (or may, of course, fail to develop in spite of the ritual). The wedding, even where it still serves as permission to consummate the relationship, can only symbolize it and announce it.

Any effort to discourage a couple who are manifestly wrong for each other is bound to have the contrary effect. But misgivings are common, especially among the inexperienced, and it may be helpful to have an occasion where they can be brought to light. In the presence of a trusted witness, commitments that have come to seem inevitable or compelled can reveal themselves as breakable, and breaks that seemed to demand impossible courage can find a way to be made. Or, through facing the contingencies of the future, the couple may discover new things to admire in each other, and become more certain that they have chosen right.

The couple should choose an experienced and thoughtful person whom they trust to read the part of the **Quintessence** *in the marriage service. They should meet with him or her at an early stage, setting aside several hours for the meeting. The questioner's role is not to judge the couple's fitness for marriage but to allow them to be fully conscious of what they think of each other.*

It may be useful for the couple to read the questions through and consider them privately, and to talk about them together—perhaps some of the time could be spent with the questioner and some without—but the presence of the third person adds a further dimension. What you say to yourself can be concealed from everyone else; what you say to your lover can be softened, or cast in your mutual private language in a way that tries to heal differences without understanding them; what you say to a third person must be fully intelligible. It should be all three people's effort to be intelligible in plain, enduring language and not in the latest curative jargon.

Partly the questions serve to reveal the lovers to each other in a setting wider than their own bond of feeling, and partly to assure them that at least one other person cares profoundly and impartially what becomes of them. Of course there should be the possibility of further appointments if the couple wishes.

Quintessence:

> You are right to fear these questions: they may be impossible to answer, and no one can know the future. But you can know, up to a point, your own means of facing difficulty, and you can know whether you understand each other's means. Do not be afraid of saying the wrong thing, or of disagreeing with each other in my presence; be afraid of the pain you will

cause each other later if you answer thoughtlessly or falsely now.

N. and N., in the marriage ceremony you will have to pledge honor. What, in your understanding, is honor?

You will be blessed with "unashamed faithfulness and unpretended love." Is there a faithfulness of which you *would* be ashamed? A love that *would* be pretended?

(*to each*) What would you most regret in your life if you did not accomplish it? Can you accomplish it while living with N.?

What can you accomplish, or become, living with N. that you could not do alone? What would you most regret if you parted from *him/her*?

What are you afraid you cannot do for N.? What are you afraid *he/she* cannot do for you?

How will you remain kind to each other in the face of lasting doubt and disappointment?

How will you remain grateful for each other?

The couple may at first be inclined to answer with abstractions—"openness and honesty," for example, may suggest much in theory but mean little in practice—and the questioner should be prepared to press for specifics. What if your lover took another lover? What if you had disagreements about money? What if one of you made much more money than the other? What if one or both of you drank too much? What if one

*of you became obsessed with some cause or activity that the other did
not understand? What if you disagreed about having children? What
if you or your lover became afraid to make love? What if some strong
inclination of yours or your lover's, not acted upon at present, became a
consuming need?—Not that anyone can have the answers mapped out
ahead of time, and the couple may well be embarrassed and angry at
such questions (not all of which will apply to them), but these ordinary
pains and calamities are where honor is lived out; if the couple can face
them seriously and painstakingly in this conversation, they will have
begun the habit of honor.*

If you think to put off doing your own work for the
other's sake, or have stopped caring about your work,
remember that you do not choose your work out of
selfishness: you choose it because it is more important
than yourself. What comes between you and your
work will harm your sense of compassion. If you can
each love the other's work while doing your own, your
compassion will flourish.

Answer this last question only to yourself, not to me.
You choose your work because of what you have suf-
fered in life: because of the things you have survived.
Is your relationship with N. worthy of what you have
survived? Answer this question only to yourself, but
if in the end you answer *no*, you must decide whether
you should still be married.

We do not require that marriage be maintained even
when it has become unbearable. But we charge you
to avoid the unbearable. The unbearable changes
you; it erodes trust from your heart and your body;
it makes you desperate. Marriage can be taken back,
but desperation cannot be taken back. Be careful of
each other.

Marriage

Nothing equals the marriage service in the old Book of Common Prayer; by comparison my own effort is excessively lyrical and lacking in austerity. Whether a marriage service ought to be austere is an open question—the Jewish service, apart from the cryptic breaking of the glass, is purely celebratory—but after an overdose of "Desiderata" and Kahlil Gibran I thought some balance of joy and sobriety was called for. "To make routine a stimulus," said Emily Dickinson, "remember it can cease": lovers who know enough to grieve in advance for each other's deaths are not likely to be susceptible to boredom.

The guests stand in a circle. In the center of the circle is a small table or altar with wine and two cups. As the processional music is played, the **Lovers** *enter the circle from opposite sides, along with five attendants representing the* **Elements**.

The **Lovers** *and the* **Quintessence** *stand at the center of the circle. The other* **Elements** *take their places in a smaller circle around the three in the center, marking the boundary of the circle with a long, bright ribbon that they pass from hand to hand. They stand so that their words go in a clockwise circle—***Earth** *at the north,* **Air** *at the east,* **Fire** *at the south, and* **Water** *at the west.*

Earth:

    The blessing of earth: the bliss of the body.

Air:

    The blessing of air: the astonishment of talk.

Fire:

> The blessing of fire: strength and health.

Water:

> The blessing of water: tears for your grief.

Quintessence:

> The blessing of the space between: that two solitudes protect and border and greet each other.
>
> It is not true that love makes all things easy; it makes us choose what is difficult. There is no rule for marriage but honor: to guard the other's integrity, and not to break trust.

Each *Lover* in turn:

> I choose what I do not see; I will fulfill what I have not promised; I promise what I cannot imagine. But I choose you, *N.*, intending you all good.

Earth:

> What is the end of desire? That nothing be lost: that your old life come whole into the new, and find rest in your lover's house.

Air:

> What is the end of desire? That the broken be mended: that the pain of your old life be healed in the new, and find solace in your lover's heart.

Fire:

> What is the end of desire? That the latent be quickened: that the sleeping powers of your old life awake in the new, and find answer in your lover's will.

Water:

> What is the end of desire? That desire be granted: that the longing of your old life be matched in the new, and find satiety in your lover's body.

Quintessence:

> What is the end of desire? Even its thwarting: for the soul you were in your old life remains in the new, and the desire of one may oppose the desire of the other. Bless even that impasse, in which you both must yield, and find honor in your lover's soul.
>
> Time is irreversible: there is no other chance at loving your lover, and the end of your bond is as sure as the beginning. Remember always the bone beneath the flesh, and that death comes to meet you on all roads:

Earth:

> Earth will rot you;

Air:

> Air will parch you;

Fire:

> Fire will scorch you;

Water:

> Water will drown you;

Quintessence:

> Sorrow will sweep you away. Will you hold to each other, even without eternity?

The Lovers answer, looking directly at each other.

First *Lover:*

> It is the mortal that gives us eternity; that which perishes is that which endures.

Second *Lover:*

> Your voice and your body are the warmth of a small fire and the light of the stars.

Quintessence:

> Then before these witnesses I marry you.

The Lovers exchange rings, each saying:

> My protection around you.

The Quintessence pours wine into the two cups, and gives them to the Lovers. Each pours a little wine into the other's cup, saying:

> My spirit within you.

They drink the wine and give the cups back to the Quintessence, who returns them to the table.

Quintessence:

> To you be intimacy and infinity; live together in unashamed faithfulness and unpretended love.

The recessional music begins, and the Lovers embrace. The Quintessence leaves the circle, and the other Elements come forward, wind the ribbon around the Lovers, and then leave the circle themselves. The Lovers unwind the ribbon and leave the circle together, the guests following.

Notes

That two solitudes protect and border and greet each other. Rainer Maria Rilke, *Letters to a Young Poet*, trans. Stephen Mitchell (New York: Random House, 1986), 78.

It is not true that love makes all things easy; it makes us choose what is difficult. Attributed to George Eliot.

Unashamed faithfulness and unpretended love. From a Byzantine monastic ceremony of spiritual brotherhood, qtd. in John Boswell, "Rediscovering Gay History: Archetypes of Gay Love in Christian History" (London: Gay Christian Movement, 1982), 19–20.

Divorce

This ritual does not take up the question of exculpation or excuse; it acknowledges the permanence of a break that has already happened, and allows both partners to face the irremediable loss of their partnership with dignity and decency. Where marriage is treated as a public triumph, divorce must inevitably be a private shame, but the decay of shared private life has public manifestations. This is one way of handling them beyond the bruising impersonality of the courtroom.

*The ritual takes place in a room with two doors. The **Partners** and the **Quintessence** stand at a table that holds a full cup of wine, two empty cups, and two pairs of scissors. The other **Elements** form a circle around them and close it by unrolling a dark ribbon hand to hand without speaking.*

Quintessence:

Who shall unmingle the wine that was mixed, or divide the living child into father and mother? What has been cannot be undone, or become as if it had not been. The separation of lovers divides them not at the point where they were joined, but jaggedly, tearing the spirit.

N. and *N.*, the time of your parting has come. Parting is not a mutual decision, as marriage is; it is a decision made in the desolation of a single heart, and if one wishes it the other can only endure it. But because even disappointed lovers must not do to each other what is unbearable, part without hatred; begin to recover the grace of solitude.

*The **Partners** may read formal statements or exchange letters to be read in private. Then each **Partner** in turn takes the full cup of wine and pours half of it into one of the empty cups, saying*:

Each *Partner:*

> The trust between us has failed, or perhaps it has never been. I release you from the pledge we did not keep.

Facing each other, they drink the wine; then they turn their backs to each other.

Earth:

> Now that you are alone, do not disdain your body.

Air:

> Now that you are alone, do not keep silence in your pain.

Fire:

> Now that you are alone, do not scorn the life you had together.

Water:

> Do not be drowned by your grief, or boiled away by your anger.

Quintessence:

> Find elsewhere hereafter unashamed faithfulness and unpretended love.

*Each **Partner** takes a pair of scissors, cuts the ribbon, and leaves the circle. They leave the room by different doors, and in such a way that they will not see each other once they are outside.*

When only one partner is present:

*Once the **Partner** has entered, the **Elements** form a circle by passing a dark ribbon hand to hand in silence. The **Quintessence** cuts the ribbon in one place.*

Quintessence:

> Who shall unmingle the wine that was mixed, or divide the living child into father and mother? What has been cannot be undone, or become as if it had not been. The separation of lovers divides them not at the point where they were joined, but jaggedly, tearing the spirit.

> N., the time of your parting from N. has come. Parting is not a mutual decision, as marriage is; it is a decision made in the desolation of a single heart, and if one wishes it the other can only endure it. But because life cannot be lived without choice, each in the end must choose the parting, and desolation give way to recovery. Part without hatred; begin to recover the grace of solitude.

*The **Partner**:*

> I declare myself free of my pledge to N., and release *him/her* from *his/her* pledge to me.

*He/she pours the wine into both of the separate cups; the **Quintessence** puts one cup outside the circle at the place where the ribbon was cut, and the **Partner** present drinks the other cup.*

Earth:

> Now that you are alone, do not disdain your body.

Air:

> Now that you are alone, do not keep silence in your pain.

Fire:

> Now that you are alone, do not scorn the life you had together.

Water:

> Do not be drowned by your grief, or boiled away by your anger.

Quintessence:

> Find elsewhere hereafter unashamed faithfulness and unpretended love.

*The **Partner** present cuts the ribbon at another place, and leaves the circle.*

Healing

I could not bring myself, in the rituals for illness and death, to maintain the structural fiction of the five elements. One does not force metaphysics on people in grief. Very likely it is impossible to achieve pure intention without metaphor, at least as long as one is using words, but if the metaphors subordinate themselves to the occasion they are at least attempting to do their job.

To be read at the sick or injured person's bedside, if he or she is strong enough and is willing (or at the family's wish if he or she is not conscious); or else in some other place.

All (*singing*):

> To Mercy, Pity, Peace, and Love,
> All pray in their distress;
> And to those virtues of delight
> Return their thankfulness.
>
> For Mercy has a human heart,
> Pity a human face,
> And Love, the human form divine,
> And Peace the human dress.

Reader:

> N., we gather for your strengthening. We know your struggle for life; we add to it our own struggle, that you not fail from us. Your body, your own place, is in danger; but the circumference of your life runs through us all, and in that wider place we stand and set our minds on your healing.

We ask for no miracle beyond the one that is given, the one that is only now called into question. The miracle is here, now: the intimate life that goes on living itself, the body in its persistence. The miracle is the intervention of our daily love between our friend and death. The miracle is the transfusion of speech and touch into the hidden realm, where they enter the leaping heart and the breathing lungs, the nested organs laboring in the dark, the blood beating under the lucent skin. We are within: from the narrow passages we look out at the distant light, and whisper along the arteries and the nerves the call that *N.*'s life calls to itself.

Each in turn:

I am.

Reader:

N.: to Mercy we pray for your life.

All:

Mercy, heal *him/her* now!

Reader:

To Pity we pray for your life.

All:

Pity, heal *him/her* now!

Reader:

To Peace we pray for your life.

All:

> Peace, heal *him/her* now!

Reader:

> To Love we pray for your life.

All:

> Love, heal *him/her* now!

*Silence is kept or songs are sung for as long as concentration can be maintained. To end the ritual the **Reader** says:*

Reader:

> Between the hammers the heart endures, as the tongue between the teeth;

All:

> And goes on praising.

Notes

To Mercy, Pity... William Blake, "The Divine Image," in *Songs of Innocence.*

[Mercy] heal her now. Numbers 12:13.

Between the hammers...and goes on praising. Rainer Maria Rilke, Ninth Duino Elegy (my translation).

Burial

The mourners bear the coffin or shrouded body to the graveside or, in bad weather, to a shelter nearby, and gather in a circle around it.

Processional Music:

> Who will take away
> Carry away sorrow,
> Bear away grief?
>
> Stream wash away
> Float away sorrow,
> Flow away, bear away
> Wear away sorrow
> Carry away grief.
>
> Mists hide away
> Shroud my sorrow,
> Cover the mountains,
> Overcloud remembrance,
> Hide away grief.
>
> Earth take away
> Make away sorrow,
> Bury the lark's bones
> Under the turf,
> Bury my grief.
>
> Black crow tear away
> Rend away sorrow,
> Talon and beak
> Pluck out the heart
> And the nerves of pain,
> Tear away grief.

Sun take away
Melt away sorrow,
Dew lies grey,
Rain hangs on the grass,
Sun dry tears.

Sleep take away
Make away sorrow,
Take away the time,
Fade away place,
Carry me away
From the world of my sorrow.

Song sigh away
Breathe away sorrow,
Words tell away,
Spell away sorrow,
Charm away grief.

Reader:

A death is the cessation of a way of being loved. Since the hour of [*time*] on [*day*], we have been without the way in which *N.* loved us. *His/her* presence is not gone, but it does not animate *his/her* body, and we are comfortless and diminished at our loss.

All:

Where is the voice that answered and the ear that heard?

They have gone out of the world, and the world has closed up behind them.

The world has closed like water over the head of our friend.

Time, that sustains the heartbeat and brings sleep
and waking,

has become the edge of a knife, severing life from
death.

Our friend is cut off in an hour that can be named,

but for us there is still the heartbeat and sleep and
waking.

Who sets the boundary for one and spares the
others?

Who sets the limit and says, This day shall be the
last?

Friend, we have given too much: what was yours in us
has died and gone with you,

and who will answer us now when we speak your
name?

Reader:

Death has taken the *man/woman*, but the name it
shall not have: names belong to the living who can
call them. (*Turns to the body and calls its name three
times.*) N.? N.? N.? (*Keeps silence.*) We call in order to
hear the silence that will answer.

All:

The absence of the dead is their way of appearing.

*As the next poem is spoken, a piece of the dead person's clothing is laid
over the body.*

All:

When you were rain you fell
when you were cup you held

when you were whole you broke
loud, loud you spoke
when you were bell

When you were way you led
homeward until the end
when you were life you died
live, live, you cried
when you were dead

Reader:

A way of speaking is dead; we can neither speak to *him/her* nor can *he/she* answer us. How shall we bear to speak about *him/her* and not to *him/her*? Yet since *he/she* is silent we must speak without *him/her*, or not at all.

Eulogies and recollections are given here.

Reader:

Wherever *he/she* is blameworthy, *he/she* is now immune to blame; wherever *he/she* is praiseworthy, *he/she* is unmoved by praise. *He/she* is no longer subject to the moral life. *He/she* has become unchanging.

To the body:

Beloved, so suddenly removed, you go where we shall follow.

All:

Your death speaks to my death through the artless words of my love.

The piece of clothing is taken up and given to the chief mourner, and the body is prepared for lowering into the grave. All hum together on one note as the next song is sung and the body is lowered. "She" should, of course, be amended to "he" for a man.

Singer:

> A slumber did my spirit seal;
>   I had no human fears;
> She seemed a thing that could not feel
>   The touch of earthly years.
>
> No motion has she now, no force;
>   She neither hears nor sees;
> Rolled round in earth's diurnal course,
>   With rocks, and stones, and trees.

Reader:

> The door is opened, and you must depart. To what? To nothing dreadful, but to the place from which you came: to things friendly and akin to you, to the elements of being. Whatever in you was fire shall go to fire; of earth, to earth; of air, to air; of water, to water. And what served the power of relation is not mortal and does not decay.

The mourners fill in the grave with earth.

Reader:

> To oblivion we were given as pasture, to perpetuate oblivion.

All:

> All that is visible clings to the invisible; the audible to the inaudible; the tangible to the intangible; perhaps

the thinkable to the unthinkable. The sun has not fallen from the sky; nor has the moon ceased from her seasons. The winds have not folded themselves up forever; nor have the clouds forgotten the chart of their aerial roads. The sea-tides have not faltered in their alternations. I am, the tree calls to the tree, and the pebble to the simple pebble.

Reader:

It is written on our hearts, the emptiness is all.

All:

That is how we have learned, the embrace is all.

Notes

Who will take away... Kathleen Raine, "Spell Against Sorrow," in *The Collected Poems of Kathleen Raine* (Washington, D.C.: Counterpoint, 2001), 71-72.

The calling of the name and the material on names, speaking and silence are adapted from Nadia Fusini's review of Jacques Derrida's *Memories of Paul de Man* (*Journal of Aesthetics and Art Criticism* 45:4, Summer 1987, 431–434).

The absence of the dead is their way of appearing. Attributed to Simone Weil.

When you were rain... Ursula K. LeGuin, "Vita Amicae," in *Hard Words* (New York: Harper and Row, 1981), 78.

Your death speaks...words of my love. Edmond Jabès, *The Book of Yukel. The Book of Questions* v. 2, trans. Rosmarie Waldrop (Middletown, CT: Wesleyan University Press, 1977), 106.

A slumber did... William Wordsworth, "A slumber did my spirit seal."

The door is opened...of water, to water. Epictetus, *Discourses* 3.13. Adapted from T. W. Rolleston's translation as quoted in John Cowper Powys, *A Philosophy of Solitude* (New York: Simon and Schuster, 1933), 22.

To oblivion...to perpetuate oblivion. Jabès, *Yukel* 114.

All that is visible...to the unthinkable. Alice Rabi Lichtenstein, "Mrs. Stein," *Sojourner, the Women's Forum* (Cambridge, MA), April 1986.

The sun has not fallen...in their alternations. Powys, *A Philosophy of Solitude, op. cit.*, 121–22.

I am, the tree calls...to the simple pebble. Jabès, *Return to the Book. The Book of Questions* v. 3, 156.

It is written...the embrace is all. Galway Kinnell, "Goodbye," in *Selected Poems* (Boston: Houghton Mifflin, 1982), 136.